THE
PATRIOTIC
CONSUMER

THE
PATRIOTIC
CONSUMER
HOW TO BUY AMERICAN

Edited by
Anne Grant and Web Burrell

Foreword by
William Lynott, Buy America Foundation

A DESIGNED FOR LIFE™ Book

Andrews and McMeel
A Universal Press Syndicate Company
Kansas City

The information contained in this work concerning the nationality of corporate entities
and country of origin of products and product parts has been derived from currently
available public documents. In some cases, we have relied on the representation and
research of other organizations and the companies themselves.

While we have made every effort to ensure the accuracy of the facts reported,
failures of disclosure, changes in corporate and brand-name ownership through merger,
acquisition, restructuring, and licensing, as well as changes in manufacturing locations
for products and product parts are constantly taking place. Therefore, no assurances
can be given as to the total or continuing accuracy of the data contained herein.

Library of Congress Cataloging-in-Publication Data

The Patriotic consumer : how to buy American / edited by Anne Grant
   and Web Burrell ; foreword by William Lynott.
        p.   cm.
    Includes bibliographical references and index.
    ISBN 0-8362-7003-7 (pbk.) : $6.95
    1. Household appliances—Purchasing. 2. Household supplies—
Purchasing. 3.Consumer education. 4. Buy national policy—
United States. I. Grant, Anne, 1952–   . II. Burrell, Web.
TX298.P39   1992
640'.73—dc20   92-34721
                                                          CIP

Book design by Barrie Maguire

CONTENTS

OUR THANKS

This book represents the contributions of many people—our writers and researchers, retail store owners and salespersons, trade association staff, corporate public relations and marketing personnel, government information officers, and foundation spokespeople.

To our writers and researchers: Joanna Pearlman, Roger Rapoport, Rich Pearlman, Alexa Barre, Vince Lupiano, Jeanne Kenney, Virginia Richard, Esq., Diane Keast, Susan Sutphin, Richard Romanski, Sharon Dauk, Bill Wagner, Stephen Scharper, and Philip Scharper—our thanks for the hundreds of hours of phone calls, statistical research, and store visits needed to write this book. Special appreciation goes to Joanna Pearlman, whose attention to detail, editorial skill, and good humor were invaluable.

We would also like to thank the following people and organizations for their help in providing information and insight concerning the issues involved in the Buy-American movement that helped to shape this book:

William Lynott, founder, Buy America Foundation; Robert Swift, Director, Cindy Sadlowski, Assistant Director, Crafted With Pride in U.S.A. Council, Inc.; George Wino, Chief Economist, American Textile Manufacturer's Institute; William Lippy, founder, Jump-Start America; Steve Eklund, Federal Trade Investigator, Federal Trade Commission; John Vanderwolf, Mary Kelly, Joanne Tucker, Joe Enright, and Ivan Shefrin, Department of Commerce (Office of Consumer Goods); Andy Kraynak and Sonja Wilson, Bureau of the Census, United States Department of Commerce; the Soap and Detergent Association; the National Housewares Association; the American Home Furnishings Association; American Furniture Manufacturing Association; Electronic Industries Association; American Home Appliance Manufacturers; Bicycle Manufacturers Association; and the Bicycle Federation of America.

Finally, our thanks to Kathleen Andrews, Tom Thornton, Donna Martin, Jean Lowe, Allan Stark, Lisa Shadid, Dorothy O'Brien, Patty Donnelly, and everyone at Andrews and McMeel who helped turn this book around in record time. A special note of thanks to Jean Lowe, our editor and champion of *The Patriotic Consumer.*

FOREWORD

Although more and more Americans are becoming aware of it, many people still do not understand the devastating damage that we are doing to our economy by our dependence on imported products.

America's gigantic trade deficit is responsible for the systematic transfer of America's wealth to our trading partners. Through our purchasing habits, we are increasing the wealth of our trading partners and raising their standard of living while we decrease our own wealth and lower our standard of living. The resulting erosion of our manufacturing base is permanently destroying millions of American jobs.

If we continue on the path that we are now following, America is destined to become an economic shell, with most American workers relegated to low-skill, low-wage service jobs.

But there is an answer. The collective American consumer is still the most powerful economic force in the world. If enough Americans are willing to follow the common-sense rule of seeking out high-quality, high-value American-made goods whenever possible, we can and will bring our foreign trade into a healthy balance.

That's why I am so pleased to see the wealth of advice and practical help offered in *The Patriotic Consumer*. Anyone interested in making a positive contribution to the restoration of America's financial well-being will find this book a dependable source of guidance and help.

WILLIAM J. LYNOTT, FOUNDER
BUY AMERICA FOUNDATION

INTRODUCTION

Americans don't need to be told to shop at home. We already know it. There's a grass-roots "BUY AMERICAN!" movement in our land that's hard to miss. This book—*The Patriotic Consumer*—was written in response to this movement. It meets an urgent need for clear background information on products and companies, so American consumers can be sure they really are buying American-made goods when they shop.

"BUY AMERICAN" isn't just bumper-sticker economics. What's going on is a serious effort to get Americans to put their money where it will help Americans the most—into American-owned companies and American-made goods.

Unfortunately, buying American isn't always as easy as it sounds. You may think you are "buying American," while the profits from your purchases are quietly being deposited in a foreign bank. In some cases, a product may be made here, but its parts are manufactured somewhere else. For certain items, an American-made alternative may not even be available. It isn't realistic to think we can buy 100 percent American. What we can do is give it our best shot.

That's where *The Patriotic Consumer* comes in. In this book, we'll give you the information you need to understand complex issues and to see what your options are. We'll help you through the maze of misleading labeling and tell you if a company is American-owned, as well as the origin of its products, parts, and labor. You can then use this information to make the choices that help America the most when you're out shopping, whether you're buying a toaster, a television, toys, or floor tiles.

The Patriotic Consumer is not out to bash foreign citizens or raise protectionist alarm calls. We're interested in what we as Americans can do to help ourselves. It's our goal to get Americans to realize that we've had the power to change the status quo all along. It's in our purses and wallets. In *The Patriotic Consumer,* we'll show how we can use our purchasing power to begin to build a better life for ourselves and our communities.

The Patriotic Consumer is organized around the classic symbol of the American dream: a typical American family home. We'll guide you through a tour of your surroundings room by room, and encourage you to take a closer look at what's around you. You'll discover the *true* origins of many of your possessions. We hope you'll then use the product information and product key available with each category in the book to make changes in your spending patterns so that you really are buying American.

The Patriotic Consumer will show you that you have good choices available to you. As you'll see in the company biographies presented in the chapter, "Made in America Hall of Fame," American ingenuity and know-how are alive and well. Great things are happening right here in the U.S. First-rate products offering real value *are* being made in America right now. Americans are hard workers and we deserve to reward ourselves for our labors. When we make each dollar we spend *really* count, we can start to buy back the American dream.

STATE OF
THE UNION

According to the Gallup poll, a majority of our citizens haven't liked what they've seen happening in America for some time. The state of the Union and the well-being of its citizens are closely linked. That's why it's so important for Americans to step back at times and take a hard look at what's going on around us. It gives us our collective sense of identity and tells us who we are as a nation, even when we don't like what we see.

We Had a Dream

It wasn't that long ago that America was the land of opportunity and optimism. You didn't have to be born rich to make it in life. All you needed was guts, determination, and a willingness to work hard. You found a good job and financial security. You bought your own home. There was the promise of an even better future for your children. The American dream was yours.

Today, Americans are faced with a different image. Poverty, unemployment, and homelessness are real concerns. Factories are closing and entire communities abandoned. Schools are overcrowded and the children in them aren't learning enough. Even the air we breathe and water we drink are suspect. No wonder people aren't satisfied with the state of the Union. Nowadays, America doesn't always look beautiful.

Somewhere along the way, we seem to have lost sight of our long-term goals. We figured cheaper was better and didn't ask questions. Where something was made wasn't quite as important as the few extra dollars in our pocket. We didn't stop to think how that might affect American jobs—or even our own lives. Now we're beginning to realize what the true costs are. Yes, some damage has been done. But the good news is that it's in our power to fix it. Let's take a look at some of the issues and at what we as patriotic consumers can do to help.

Where Have All the Good Jobs Gone?

The cornerstone of the American dream has always been a good job. Americans want to work in productive, needed jobs that pay a living wage. In the fourth quarter of 1991, more than a million American workers were classified as "discouraged." These are people who *want* jobs but who have given up hope of finding suitable employment. Suitable employment doesn't mean a dead-end service job with low pay and no benefits. Flipping burgers may be okay as a teen-ager's first work experience, but it's sure no way to support a family and pay off a mortgage.

Over the years, there has been a change in the type of work Americans do. We've seen the number of manufacturing jobs decline, replaced by jobs in the service sector. In 1946, 41 percent of nonfarm employment was in the goods-producing sector. In 1980, the goods-producing sector accounted for 28 percent of nonfarm employment. By 1990, it was only 23 percent. American manufacturing jobs are being eliminated as U.S. factories close and companies move their production facilities to foreign soil to take advantage of cheap labor and a more favorable regulatory climate.

By buying American-made goods, we can let manufacturers know that we want the jobs to stay at home. Putting our money into American companies in turn encourages those companies to invest in new factories and equipment. This improves workers' productivity, which means increased wages and a higher standard of living.

Jobs are created when workers are needed to build the factories and provide the equipment and raw materials to make the goods that are in demand. More jobs are created when the workers spend their wages on housing and automobiles and household goods for themselves. Unemployment goes down when the country's economy experiences strong and steady growth. It's up to us as patriotic consumers to help spur that growth.

Hey, Mister, Can You Spare a Buck?

One part of the American dream that goes hand in hand with a good job is financial security. That security now seems a thing of the past. We may remember the stories our parents and grandparents told us about bread lines during the Great Depression of the 1930s. We may have weathered some past recessions ourselves. Now we're facing a Recession with a capital "R." Nobody wants to use the "D" word, but who'd have thought we'd ever live to see the day when people were once again reduced to standing on street corners holding cardboard signs that read "Will work for food!"

How did we ever get into such a mess? We were caught by surprise. Americans borrowed against tomorrow thinking the good times would never end. (Ever wonder how many of the things we bought during those good times were foreign-made?) The result—people who'd been living on the edge are now over it. In 1981, there were 360,329 bankruptcy petitions filed in the United States. In 1989, bankruptcies were up nearly 80 percent to 642,993. In a study of poverty levels among eight industrial nations during the 1980s, only the United States came in with double-digit figures for adults, children, and the elderly. According to the U.S. Bureau of the Census, as of March 1991, 12.8 percent of all Americans were living below the poverty level. Many are people who once had jobs and savings and a sense of security. People who believed in the American dream.

What can we do? Anything that gets American workers productive employment is going to be good for all of us. People with jobs pay taxes. Men and women who have good jobs don't burden the welfare system. Workers who earn a fair living can afford to pay their bills. Employees who receive decent benefits, such as health care coverage and a pension plan, can feel more secure about their futures. At a time when the middle class appears to be shrinking and the average age of Americans is on the rise, we need to do all we can to get people to work and improve the tax base. Only then can we begin to ensure our own futures.

There's No Place Like Home

Shelter is right up there with food and clothing as a basic human necessity. It's a need that for many Americans isn't being met. For them, the American dream of a comfortable home has been replaced by an ongoing search for shelter of any kind.

Go into the public library in any major American city and you're likely to find it being used by the homeless as a daytime refuge. We see homeless persons everywhere—riding the buses and subways, living under bridges and in vacant buildings. When the weather's nice, they live in the parks and plazas and even set up tent cities. Who are they?

Homeless Americans today are no different from us, except maybe a little less lucky. They're not the skid-row types, the drinkers and drifters and mental cases we tend to associate with homelessness. Sure, there are plenty of homeless single men. But there are also homeless women of all ages, married couples, even entire families with children. How did this happen?

The reason many Americans are homeless is that housing costs are rising faster than incomes. It's more and more difficult for many of us to meet our mortgages or pay our rents when they can take as much as half our monthly income or more. Foreclosures and evictions are way up. Just getting the deposit money together for an apartment can be beyond the reach of many people.

The solution is in affordable housing—with *affordable* being the key word. For very low-income Americans that may mean subsidized rents or room vouchers. (In the last ten years, federal spending for subsidized housing adjusted for inflation was down 82 percent.)

But for most people, housing will be affordable when wages are high enough to cover it and the other basics and still leave a comfortable margin left over for emergencies. People with decent jobs can afford decent housing. By buying American, we can encourage business and industry to create those decent jobs.

The Next Generation

In 1965, 10 percent of the nation's children lived in poverty. Today, it's closer to 25 percent. More than half of these children live in single-parent households. Often they don't have access to adequate medical care or a quality education. How can we promise our children a better future when we can't even take care of them today?

While buying American-made products can't cure all the underlying social problems that create broken homes, investment in education and job training and the availability of high-paying jobs can help break the cycle of poverty. A welfare mother can't afford to give up her benefits for a service job that doesn't pay enough to cover the cost of a babysitter, let alone rent and groceries. But offer an opportunity for training and the promise of a decent job, and more than likely she'll jump at the chance to rise above her situation.

The American dream is about self-worth and the value of the individual as a contributing member of society. The future depends on a literate, well-educated, well-trained work force. Investing in our children and their parents is the safest bet we can make.

Give U.S. a Chance

You've heard the excuses people have for not buying American-made goods. They'll tell you it's because our products aren't well-made or the price isn't competitive. They'll say American workers are lazy and have a bad attitude. Well, that's just not the case. Let's dispel the myths right now and look at the facts.

MYTH: American workers are lazy. FACT: We are working longer than ever. There are more hours in the average American work year now than there were back in the 1950s. Only the Japanese take less vacation time than we do.

MYTH: American workers aren't productive. FACT: We are working harder than ever. American industrial output increased 29 percent in the last decade. American workers are the most productive, when compared to the workers of other industrialized nations. Our workers overall are 30 percent more productive than Japanese workers.

MYTH: American products aren't well-made. FACT: We are working better than ever. The American work ethic is intact and there's a wide range of high-quality American-made products around to prove it. We are the inventors and innovators who are always trying to build that better mousetrap.

CONCLUSION: The American worker is not the problem. Productivity rises with training and modern technology. Americans created much of the technology of the twentieth century. We could also be the creators of the technology of the twenty-first century, if we encourage tax breaks for research and development and capital investment in new factories and infrastructure—our roads and bridges, transportation, and communication systems.

We need to convince business and government that we're in it for the long term, not just the next quarter's bottom line. In the chapter "The Patriotic Citizen," we'll give you some tips on how you can make your opinions known and encourage change.

Dream the Possible Dream

We don't have to be the first generation of Americans to live in a "post-American" era. Some might say that as a people we've grown complacent and a bit soft around the edges. Maybe it's true, but, to paraphrase Mark Twain, "Reports of our death have been greatly exaggerated."

What Americans need to do to get back on track is to understand what our goals are. As a nation, we've often done what wasn't thought possible, because we *believed* we could do it. Could it be we had a clearer vision of ourselves when our goals were to push our frontier westward, building railroads and settling the country? Despite our mistakes, we created a strong, diverse, and vital society—a model of democracy the world over. Maybe we were more focused when we were aiming at the moon. Now, we've been to the moon and back again. Where do we go next?

Let's look at ourselves as a new breed of pioneer. While past generations built America, our mission can be to rebuild it. American spirit, energy, talent, and determination still exist. It's within our power to take control of our lives and to help ourselves. By investing in America today, we can create a new frontier and open up unlimited possibilities for the future—we can rediscover the American dream and make it our reality.

WELCOME TO
OUR HOME

From the time the very first pilgrims arrived and began to settle this land, the American family home has been at the core of the American dream. For this reason, we've chosen to use a model of the typical modern American home as a way to organize product information in an entertaining and usable format. In the following section, you'll find that we've divided our "home" into seven rooms (including the garage), and given each room its own chapter. Each chapter offers some general product history, as well as information and recommendations about specific items. For instance, you'll find refrigerators and pots and pans in the kitchen chapter, clothing and linens in the bedroom chapter, toys and home electronics in the family room chapter, and cars and sporting goods in the garage chapter. If you want to locate an item quickly and aren't sure what room to find it in, the contents page has an itemized list of the major categories.

The Patriotic Consumer is an *introduction* to buying American products. Use it as a resource guide and reference. Keep it in the glove compartment of your car and take it with you when you go shopping. But remember, it's not meant to be all-inclusive, just a place to start. We aren't trying to tell you how you should spend your dollars because there is no one right answer. (As we mentioned earlier, sometimes there isn't even going to be a completely American option, and your best choice may be to buy a product that was manufactured overseas by an American-owned company.) Our goal is simply to give you the best possible information so you can go out and make an informed decision when you shop. We *will* tell you about current trends and buying patterns, and give you the most recent information about a product available at the time this book went to press. But, because manufacturers are always shifting production locales, and company ownership can change so quickly in this era of leveraged buyouts and takeovers, you'll still need to read labels carefully and ask questions when you shop.

A brief word about our American Buying Power product key: at the end of each product category, you'll find a list of brand names. Grouped with product names, you'll find American flags and partial flags, that tell you at a glance whether a brand is American-owned, if it is American-made, and whether its component parts originated in this country. For our product key research, we used a Federal Trade Commission law that requires any product marked "Made in the USA" to be manufactured with 100 percent American parts and labor. If a product contains less than 50 percent American parts and labor, the country of origin must be labeled. The country-of-origin label is optional if a product contains more than 50 percent but less than 100 percent American parts and labor. For the purposes of our product key, we're calling a company American-owned if the net profits remain in this country.

Look at the following product key for Vacuums. By looking at the flags, you can tell at a glance whether a product is:

100% American made and owned;

American-owned, and over 50% American parts and/or labor;

American-owned, using less than 50% American parts and/or labor;

Foreign-owned, using American parts and/or labor;

Foreign-owned, foreign parts and/or labor.

VACUUM CLEANERS

100% American made and owned:

- Royal® Dirt Devil® Series 500®
- Hoover® Spectrum™
- Hoover® Power Max™

American-owned, and over 50% American parts and/or labor:

- Black & Decker® PowerPro™ Dustbuster Plus™
- Black & Decker® Dustbuster Upright Power Brush™
- Sunbeam

American-owned, using less than 50% American parts and/or labor:

- Hoover (some models assembled in Mexico)
- Sears Kenmore (some models)
- Sunbeam (some models)

Foreign-owned, using American parts and/or labor:

- Eureka Powerline™ Gold 5.0 peak horsepower
- Eureka Mighty Mite® The Boss®
- Eureka Ultra™ upright vacuum cleaner

Foreign-owned, foreign parts and/or labor:

- Eureka Hand-Held Vacuums
- Eureka "Stick" Brooms
- Panasonic

NOTE: As you go through the Product Keys, don't be confused if you don't find products listed under every icon grouping. In some cases, we found that there were products that did not fit into each of the five groupings. For example, there are no videocassette recorders being manufactured in the United States by either an American or an American-owned overseas company.

As a patriotic consumer, *where* you shop is just as important as what brand you buy. Before you set out on your next shopping expedition, consider the ownership of your favorite department or specialty store. Listed on the next page are some of the major retailers in America, and who owns them—some will probably surprise you.

American Retailers
- Ames
- Banana Republic
- Bergdorf Goodman
- Broadway
- Caldor
- Costco
- Dayton Hudson
- Dollar General
- Emporium Capwell's
- Family Dollar
- The Gap
- G. Fox
- Hecht's
- Home Depot
- I. Magnin
- Ivey's
- Jacobson's Stores
- Kay-Bee Toy and Hobby
- K mart
- Liberty House
- The Limited
- Lord & Taylor
- Macy's
- Marshalls
- Marshall Fields
- Mervyns
- Montgomery Ward
- Neiman-Marcus
- Nordstrom's
- J.C. Penney
- Sears
- True Value

Foreign Retailers
- Abraham & Straus (Canada)
- Allied Stores (Canada)
- Anne Klein & Co. (Japan)
- Benetton (Italy)
- Black, Starr, and Frost (England)
- Bloomingdale's (Canada)
- Bonwit Teller (Australia)
- Brooks Brothers (England)
- Bullocks (Canada)
- Burdine's (Canada)
- FAO Schwartz (Netherlands)
- Foxmoor (Canada)
- Garfinkel's (Saudi Arabia)
- Herman's Sporting Goods (England)
- Jordan Marsh (Canada)
- Kay Jewelers (England)
- Korvettes (France)
- Laura Ashley (England)
- Lazarus (Canada)
- Loehmann's Inc. (Spain)
- Maas Brothers (Canada)
- Ohrbach's (Netherlands)
- Rich's (Canada)
- Saks Fifth Avenue (Bahrain)
- 7-Eleven (Japan)
- Stern's (Canada)
- Talbots (Japan)
- Zale's (Canada/Switzerland)

Now, you may want to put on your walking shoes and get ready to take a fresh look at your surroundings . . . because it's time to start our house tour.

THE KITCHEN

The kitchen is as American as Mom and apple pie. It's the center of the action, the very heart and soul of a home, and it reflects our personal taste as much as any room in our house. Like the traditional hearth, the kitchen is the informal gathering place for family and friends. No wonder, then, that it's unsettling to look around this center of family life and find so many products from abroad.

Take an Inventory

In 1959 at a Moscow exhibition, then Vice President Richard Nixon and Soviet Premier Nikita Khrushchev debated in front of a model of the typical American kitchen. Ever since, this room has symbolized our unique way of life. How ironic, then, that so many of the wonderful conveniences found in our kitchens today are made on foreign shores. It doesn't have to be that way! Let's begin with a look at those familiar kitchen appliances in your own home.

Maybe you're the kind of shopper who did your homework in *Consumer Reports*, searched for the best energy rating, and then waited to buy until the price plummeted in a super sale. Good work. But how much do you know about the company behind the label? Now is a good time to take an inventory of your refrigerator, stove, microwave oven, countertop appliances, dishes, and silverware. And don't forget the floor covering. Jot down the names of the manufacturers and you've taken the first step toward becoming a more patriotic consumer.

Don't Be Fooled

We may think the easiest way to buy American products is to choose familiar domestic brands. Just looking at the nameplate, though, won't always tell you who really built the product. For example, Frigidaire, one of the best-known American refrigerator lines, is owned by the Swedish firm Electrolux. Many appliance manufacturers give an American address without mentioning where their products are made. If your coffee grinder is a General Electric, you should know that it was actually made by Sunbeam in the Far East. If you have an RCA microwave, you may be surprised to learn that it was built by General Electric at a Samsung factory in Korea.

Comparison Shopping

You know buying American helps our economy. But did you know it can also help your pocketbook? You'll be pleased to hear American kitchen appliances, housewares, and fixtures are often the best value on the market. Many of the most energy-efficient models are made in our country. American manufacturers use state-of-the-art electrical safety technology and avoid dangerous practices common in some foreign-made goods, such as the use of lead-based paint on pottery.

The Payoff

From the time of the very first settlers, Americans have gathered around the family hearth to share companionship, food, and warmth. That tradition continues in the kitchens of today. As the center of family life, the kitchen is a great place to start as we begin to buy back the American dream.

• Experts estimate that Americans will replace roughly 6.4 million toasters in 1992. If everyone purchased a $30 American-made replacement toaster, 4,800 new jobs could be created in the appliance industry.

• If 40 American households each spent $1,000 on American-made products for the kitchen, instead of imports, a new job could be created for an American worker.

Large Appliances

Each year Americans buy more than 24 million major kitchen appliances. From the three-door refrigerator to the countertop microwave, you'll find a bewildering array of choices. How about a gas or electric range? Do you need a rotisserie feature on your microwave? Should you buy a dishwasher with a booster heater? Would a built-in refrigerator work best? So many decisions! Yet many consumers forget to ask the most important question of all: Was the appliance made in our country by a domestic manufacturer? As you'll see on the following pages, many of the best models are 100 percent American-made.

Small Appliances

While foreign manufacturers dominate much of the small-appliance market, it's not hard to buy American. High-quality toasters, coffee makers, and food processors are all made domestically. Although foreign products may be a few dollars cheaper, you'll often find the American products have better warranties and service plans. In addition, it's often easier to find parts when you need them. Several American manufacturers also offer impressive safety features, such as exterior trim that won't conduct heat.

REFRIGERATORS

Long gone are the days of the iceman. Nowadays, it's easy to chill out. With annual sales of more than 8.5 million units, refrigerators and freezers are the top-selling major kitchen appliances. You can choose among a freestanding two- or three-door model, a unit with the freezer on the bottom, or a built-in. If you own an older model, note that the lower energy costs on a new unit may actually pay for your purchase within 7 to 10 years. Many of the most efficient models are 100 percent American-made.

American Buying Pattern

- Every year, we buy 6.8 million refrigerators worth about $4.8 billion.
- Californians buy more than 10 percent of the refrigerators sold in the United States.
- The annual electricity bill for the average American frost-free refrigerator is $120.
- Beginning in 1993, refrigerators will consume at least 25 percent less energy, due to the National Appliance Energy Conservation Act. That means that a typical refrigerator will not consume as much energy as a 100-watt light bulb!
- Ninety percent of Americans own refrigerators that are either white or almond in color.
- More than 60 percent of the refrigerators in American households are frost-free.

REFRIGERATORS

100% American made and owned:

- Amana® 24-inch space-saving refrigerator/freezer
- Amana® Free-O'-Frost™ side-by-side refrigerator/freezer
- Amana® side-by-side with ice dispenser
- Amana® Bottom Mount Refrigerator

American-owned, and over 50% American parts and/or labor:

- Whirlpool side-by-side refrigerator/freezer
- Kenmore side-by-side refrigerator/freezer
- KitchenAid® Superba side-by-side refrigerator/freezer
- Capri side-by-side refrigerator/freezer
- Kenmore refrigerator with top freezer
- Maytag refrigerator with top freezer
- General Electric side-by-side refrigerator/freezer
- Whirlpool refrigerator with bottom freezer

American-owned, using less than 50% American parts and/or labor:

- General Electric Compact Refrigerator
- Welbilt 2-door refrigerator/freezer

Foreign-owned, using American parts and/or labor:

- White-Westinghouse Frost Free side-by-side
- White-Westinghouse Frost Free refrigerator with top freezer
- Frigidaire
- Gibson
- Tappan

Foreign-owned, foreign parts and/or labor

RANGES

While free-standing ranges are the leading choice of American consumers, built-ins are growing in popularity. Besides the traditional electric and gas ranges, you may want to consider high-tech alternatives like halogen and smooth-top ceramic glass burners. Serious cooks may opt for a commercial-style unit that provides more BTUs. Whether you choose a mass-market or custom unit, you'll be happy to know that American-made ranges can be state of the art.

American Buying Pattern

- Each year Americans buy about 5 million ranges, worth roughly $2.5 billion in sales.
- On the average, Americans keep their appliances 11 to 15 years.
- Most major home appliances have become more energy-efficient since 1972.

RANGES (ELECTRIC)

100% American made and owned:

- Magic Chef® Self-Cleaning Oven/Automatic Cooking
- Magic Chef® Electronic Control

American-owned, and over 50% American parts and/or labor:

- Kenmore 30-inch Electric Range with Porcelain Oven
- General Electric 30-inch Electric Range with Porcelain Oven
- Capri 30-inch Electric Range with Porcelain Oven
- Whirlpool 30-inch Electric Range with Self-Cleaning Oven
- Jenn-Aire® 30-inch Electric Griller with Slide-in Range
- Lady Kenmore
- General Electric 30-inch Griller
- Caloric Prestige Series Self-Cleaning Oven
- Whirlpool Designer Style Self-Cleaning Oven

American-owned, using less than 50% American parts and/or labor

Foreign-owned, using American parts and/or labor:

- Tappan Self-Cleaning Oven
- Electrolux (WCI)

Foreign-owned, foreign parts and/or labor

RANGES (GAS)

100% American made and owned:

- Magic Chef® Electronic Control with Sealed Burners
- Magic Chef® with Uniburners

American-owned, and over 50% American parts and/or labor:

- Capri 30-inch Gas Range with Porcelain Oven
- Caloric Prestige Series

American-owned, using less than 50% American parts and/or labor:

- General Electric 30-inch Free-Standing Gas Range
- General Electric XL44
- Kenmore 30-inch with self-cleaning oven
- General Electric Self-Cleaning Oven with Electronic Ignition

Foreign-owned, using American parts and/or labor:

- Tappan Self-Cleaning Oven with Electronic Ignition
- Electrolux (WCI)

Foreign-owned, foreign parts and/or labor

MICROWAVE OVENS

Far too often, the history of innovation in our nation falls into three distinct stages. First, a brilliant inventor makes an astonishing technical breakthrough. Second, an American company spends millions of dollars developing and selling the new creation to the masses. Finally, after the idea has proven its worth, a foreign competitor sweeps in, reverse-engineers the product, and dominates the American market.

Exhibit A is the microwave oven. At the end of World War II, an engineer at Raytheon accidentally placed a bag of popcorn next to a microwave unit that was part of a radar system. The kernels promptly popped and the company quickly realized the culinary possibilities. But it wasn't until the mid-sixties, when Raytheon took over the venerable Amana Refrigeration Company, that the Radarange began to move out of the restaurant and institutional markets into the general American consumer market.

Today, five Asian companies—Samsung, Goldstar, Sharp, Matsushita, and Sanyo—dominate this market. Inventor Raytheon has a mere 5 percent share of the American microwave market and is better known for defending Israel with Patriot missiles than for selling ovens that zap TV dinners. While some of the best-selling American brands are made abroad, the good news is that we have the buying power to reverse this trend.

American Buying Pattern

- Americans spend $2.5 billion annually on 10.8 million microwave ovens.
- Roughly 4 out of 5 units are made abroad.
- The average microwave oven lasts for 11 years.
- Most of the microwave sales today are for replacement units, and experienced buyers are passing over models with a variety of functions and power levels in favor of models that are simple to operate.

MICROWAVE OVENS

100% American made and owned:

- Amana® Radarange® Touchmatic

American-owned, and over 50% American parts and/or labor

American-owned, using less than 50% American parts and/or labor:

- Caloric® Microwave
- Magic Chef® MVP III
- General Electric Spacemaker II
- General Electric Turntable Microwave Oven
- Kenmore Solid State
- Amana® Radarange® 650 watts

Foreign-owned, using American parts and/or labor:

- Tappan 750-watt, features Browning Element
- Tappan Speed Wave 1000
- Tappan Turnabout
- Quasar Midsize
- Sharp® Carousel® II
- Panasonic® Mid-Size Microwave Oven
- Frigidaire

Foreign-owned, foreign parts and/or labor:

- Panasonic® Large Capacity
- Samsung Classic Collection II

DISHWASHERS

Great news! Many of the top-rated dishwashers are American-made. Whether you choose a built-in or portable unit, a compact model or a standard design, there's no problem finding an economical, power-saving dishwasher that's been built in our country. American dishwashers have a reputation for dependability, with an average life expectancy of 10 years. No wonder our leading manufacturers are so successful selling this appliance abroad.

American Buying Pattern

- Americans buy 3.5 million dishwashers annually.
- Almost all of them are made in the United States.
- Fifty-one percent of American homes have a dishwasher.
- It costs about $70 a year to run a dishwasher.
- The average dishwasher lasts 10 years.

DISHWASHERS

100% American made and owned:

- KitchenAid® Automatic Water Heating Quiet Scrub
- KitchenAid® 24-inch Built-in Dishwasher
- KitchenAid® 24-inch Automatic Water Heating
- In-Sink-Erator Classic Supreme

American-owned, and over 50% American parts and/or labor:

- Maytag Jetclean Dishwasher
- Whirlpool Quiet Wash System
- General Electric Potscrubber 660
- General Electric Potscrubber 720
- General Electric Potscrubber 1120
- Magic Chef® with Super Scrub II
- Kenmore 24-inch Built-in Dishwasher
- Kenmore Ultra Wash II
- Whirlpool 24-inch Dishwasher
- General Electric Twenty-Eight Hundred

American-owned, using less than 50% American parts and/or labor

Foreign-owned, using American parts and/or labor:

- White-Westinghouse Filter Clean System, Sound Insulated
- Electrolux (WCI)

Foreign-owned, foreign parts and/or labor:

- Bosch dishwasher

WASHERS AND DRYERS

America's sure not washed up in this department! Not only is the market for washers and dryers safely in American hands, our companies are moving ahead impressively overseas. Nearly all of the 10.5 million washers and dryers purchased in this country are made here.

One company, Whirlpool, has half the market. Whirlpool's corporate predecessor began making washing machines for the Sears catalog in 1916. It wasn't until 1948 that the company chose to market washers under the Whirlpool name. The firm went on to launch a complete appliance line. Through European and Asian subsidiaries, the company now has foreign sales of more than $2.7 billion. Other major players known for their durable product lines are Maytag, General Electric, and Speed Queen.

American Buying Pattern

- Americans buy 10.5 million washers and dryers annually.
- Eighty percent of American homes have a washer/dryer.
- United States exports of washers, dryers and other household appliances have nearly doubled since 1986.
- Major markets for American exports are Mexico, Japan, Canada, and Taiwan.
- In over 90 percent of American families, female heads of household still do the laundry.

WASHERS

100% American made and owned

American-owned, and over 50% American parts and/or labor:

- Magic Chef® 20-pound capacity Heavy Duty
- Maytag Selfclean Filter, Large Capacity
- KitchenAid® Two-Speed Quiet Scrub Washer
- Kenmore 80 series Heavy Duty Washer
- Whirlpool Heavy Duty Six-Cycle Washer
- Kenmore 70 series Heavy-Duty Washer
- Whirlpool 7-cycle washer
- KitchenAid® Superba Three-Speed
- Lady Kenmore 15-cycle washer

American-owned, using less than 50% American parts and/or labor

Foreign-owned, using American parts and/or labor:

- Frigidaire
- Gibson
- Tappan
- White-Westinghouse

Foreign-owned, foreign parts and/or labor

DRYERS
(GAS AND ELECTRIC)

100% American made and owned

American-owned, and over 50% American parts and/or labor:

- General Electric Five-Cycle Automatic Dryer
- Whirlpool Large Capacity Automatic Dry Miser
- Whirlpool Super Capacity 2-speed 8-cycle
- Maytag End of Cycle Signal
- Whirlpool Large Capacity Supreme
- KitchenAid® Superba
- Lady Kenmore
- KitchenAid® Extra Capacity/Heavy-Duty
- Whirlpool Gas Dryer Large Capacity
- Speed Queen Marathon Heavy-Duty Dryer

American-owned, using less than 50% American parts and/or labor

Foreign-owned, using American parts and/or labor:

- White-Westinghouse Heavy-Duty
- Frigidaire
- Gibson
- Tappan

Foreign-owned, foreign parts and/or labor

TOASTERS

This product has come a long way from the basic chrome two-slice model that many of us grew up with. Special features now include speed toasting and handy bread warmers. A built-in model is an option to the more traditional stand-alone unit. And, best of all, you can still buy American. Some companies, like Sunbeam, not only make their own toasters here, they buy nearly all the components domestically. An American company, Proctor-Silex, is the world's top toaster manufacturer.

American Buying Pattern

- Approximately 95 percent of American homes have toasters on their countertops.
- More than ten million toasters were shipped in 1991. Of these, 29 percent were Toastmaster, 16 percent Black & Decker, and 7 percent Sunbeam.
- American manufacturers exported over 950,000 toasters in 1990, at a value of more than $14 million.
- On the average, a toaster lasts 11 years.

TOASTERS (2-SLICE)

100% American made and owned:

- Toastmaster® Quick Toaster™
- Toastmaster® Deluxe Bakery 2-slice Toaster
- Toastmaster® Wide Slot Pastry Toaster
- Proctor-Silex® Shade-Tronic™ Toast Memory
- Sears Kenmore 2-slice Toaster
- Proctor-Silex® Shade-Tronic Lot-A-Slot™ 2-slice toaster
- Hamilton Beach–Proctor-Silex 2-slice toaster

American-owned, and over 50% American parts and/or labor

American-owned, using less than 50% American parts and/or labor:

- Rival® 2-slice toaster
- Waring 2-slice toaster
- Sunbeam Electronic 2-slice toaster
- Black & Decker® 2-slice Cool Touch toaster
- Black & Decker® FasToast 2-slice toaster

Foreign-owned, using American parts and/or labor:

- Farberware 2-slice toaster

Foreign-owned, foreign parts and/or labor

TOASTERS (4-SLICE)

100% American made and owned:

- Proctor-Silex Bread Brain Deluxe Bread Pastry Toaster
- Toastmaster® Under Cabinet 4-slice toaster
- Toastmaster® Cool Steel™ Wide Slot Toaster
- Toastmaster® Toasters Choice
- Toastmaster® 4-slice toaster #D126
- Toastmaster® 4-slice toaster #D149

American-owned, and over 50% American parts and/or labor

American-owned, using less than 50% American parts and/or labor:

- Black & Decker®
- Sunbeam/Oster
- Procter-Silex

Foreign-owned, using American parts and/or labor:

- Farberware 4-slice toaster

Foreign-owned, foreign parts and/or labor

TOASTER OVENS

100% American made and owned:

- Proctor-Silex® Ovenmaster™ Toaster Oven/Broiler
- Proctor-Silex® Ovenmaster™ Toaster Oven/Broiler
- Toastmaster® 6-slice Toaster-Oven Broiler

American-owned, and over 50% American parts and/or labor:

- Black & Decker® Toast-R-Oven,™ TRO400
- Sears Kenmore Electronic Toaster Oven/Broiler
- Black & Decker® Toast-R-Oven™ and Broiler
- Black & Decker® Toast-R-Oven,™ TRO500

American-owned, using less than 50% American parts and/or labor

Foreign-owned, using American parts and/or labor

Foreign-owned, foreign parts and/or labor:

- DeLonghi "Alfredo De Lux"

COFFEE MAKERS

What could be more American than a cup of French roast to start the day? Especially if it's made in a sleek German coffee maker. It doesn't have to be that way.

You can choose ground beans from the sun-drenched fields of Kona, Hawaii, and brew them in your choice of space-saving American-made units that come complete with digital timers and handy carafes. From low-end units to space-age designs that will halt brewing to let you pour yet another cup, American manufacturers are highly competitive. Some of the biggest companies—like Mr. Coffee—divide their manufacturing between domestic and foreign plants. We're here to help straighten out the confusion.

American Buying Pattern

- Each year we buy more than 12.7 million coffee makers.
- American-made Black & Decker ranks second in the domestic market.
- Drip-type coffee makers are the most popular model, selling more than 9.5 million units in 1990, a dollar value of more than $200 million.
- On average, a drip coffee maker will last 4 years.

COFFEE MAKERS

100% American made and owned:

- Mr. Coffee 10-cup auto drip coffeemaker
- Mr. Coffee Accel
- Mr. Coffee The Expert
- Regal 4–8-cup Poly Perk®
- Regal 5-cup Poly Hot Pot
- West Bend® 12–30-cup Party Perk

American-owned, and over 50% American parts and/or labor:

- Black & Decker 10-cup Compact
- Black & Decker 10-cup Spacemaker Drip Coffeemaker

American-owned, using less than 50% American parts and/or labor:

- Regal 4–10-cup drip coffeemaker
- Proctor-Silex 2–12-cup Auto drip
- Kenmore 2–12-cup Auto Drip Coffeemaker
- Mr. Coffee 10-cup compact coffee maker
- Presto 2–12-cup Stainless Steel Coffee Maker
- Braun 12-cup Aromaster
- Toastmaster 10-cup coffeemaker

Foreign-owned, using American parts and/or labor

Foreign-owned, foreign parts and/or labor:

- Singer 5 'n 1 Coffee Maker
- N.A.P. (Norelco)
- Krups

FOOD PROCESSORS

Would it surprise you to learn that the trend-setting Cuisinart is made in America . . . by an American-owned company? When shopping for a food processor, you'll find that many of the top-rated units are built right here and the price is right. With prices ranging from about $30 to nearly $400, you'll easily find a model to fit your budget. Even the original 1936 Waring Blendor is being sold as a collector's item through the Williams-Sonoma catalog for about $120.

A great time-saver, these units can help you knead dough for bread or make your own baby food. By combining the functions of many other kitchen appliances, food processors can also save a lot of space. You'll find that a number of the moderately priced American units hold their own against the higher priced imports.

American Buying Pattern

- Americans manufactured over a million food processors in 1990, a value of more than $24 million.
- Exports of household food preparation appliances in 1990 topped 400,000 units, valued at more than $10 million.
- Experts estimate that more than 3 million food processors will need to be replaced in 1992.

FOOD PROCESSORS

100% American made and owned:

- Regal® La Machine® II
- Cuisinart® Food Processor Model DLC-5
- Oster Kitchen Center®

American-owned, and over 50% American parts and/or labor

American-owned, using less than 50% American parts and/or labor:

- Sears Kenmore 6-speed Food Processor
- Sunbeam Oskar Food Processor
- Betty Crocker® Power Chop™ Micro Food Processor
- Cuisinart Mini-prep™ Processor

Foreign-owned, using American parts and/or labor:

- Hamilton Beach® Dual Speed Food Processor

Foreign-owned, foreign parts and/or labor:

- Krups Mini Pro Processor
- Moulinex®

VACUUM CLEANERS

If you were born in the 1950s, there's a good chance that your mother referred to vacuuming as "Hoovering." Based in North Canton, Ohio, the Hoover Company produces a wide selection of models that include the best-selling upright in America for more than 30 years, the Hoover Convertible. Priced from under $100 to around $400, you'll be sure to find one that's just right for your home, and your budget.

If longevity is one of your criteria in choosing a vacuum cleaner, you'll want to check out the Electrolux (the vacuum division is still an American company), made in Marietta, Georgia, which is designed to last for 20 years. Its reputation for high quality carries a price that starts at around $300 for an upright model.

Quality is what Eureka vacuum cleaners are all about, too. Returns on warranty are less than 1 percent, and almost all of their vacuums are made in the United States. Unfortunately, however, Eureka is no longer an American-owned company.

It's hard to believe that it has been over 10 years since Black & Decker created the Dustbuster. This handy cordless cleaner is an essential part of many American households, and a popular gift item as well.

American Buying Pattern

- More than 98 percent of American households own at least one vacuum, with 20 percent owning three or more vacuum cleaners.
- Approximately 11 million full-sized vacuum cleaners were sold in 1991. Hand-held vacuums accounted for an additional 6 million units sold last year.
- The entire electric floor care market accounts for more than $2.5 billion in sales each year.

VACUUM CLEANERS

100% American made and owned:

- Royal® Dirt Devil® Series 500®
- Hoover® Spectrum™
- Hoover® Power Max™
- Royal® Dirt Devil® Upright™
- Hoover® Legacy Heavy Duty
- Kenmore Cannister vacuum cleaner
- Electrolux Ultralux® LXE cannister vacuum cleaner
- Electrolux Diplomat® LXE cannister vacuum cleaner
- Electrolux Genesis LXE upright vacuum cleaner
- Hoover Power Max
- Hoover Elite II
- Oreck XL

American-owned, and over 50% American parts and/or labor:

- Black & Decker® PowerPro™ Dustbuster Plus™
- Black & Decker® Dustbuster Upright Power Brush™
- Sunbeam

American-owned, using less than 50% American parts and/or labor:

- Hoover (some models assembled in Mexico)
- Sears Kenmore (some models)
- Sunbeam (some models)

Foreign-owned, using American parts and/or labor:

- Eureka Powerline™ Gold 5.0 peak horsepower
- Eureka Mighty Mite® The Boss®
- Eureka Ultra™ upright vacuum cleaner
- Eureka Commercial Type B
- White-Westinghouse
- Regina

Foreign-owned, foreign parts and/or labor:

- Eureka Hand-Held Vacuums
- Eureka "Stick" Brooms
- Panasonic
- Sharp
- Rexair

COOKWARE

If your mother or father cooked dinner in Revere Ware every night, you need no introduction to American cookware. With hundreds of companies making state-of-the-art pots and pans, skillets, bakeware, and utensils, it's easy to buy at home. Not only is American-made cookware more affordable, it is also the first choice of many home and professional kitchen designers.

American Buying Power

- American manufacturers of stamped and cast aluminum cookware reported sales of $305 million in 1991.
- Stainless steel cookware sales were approximately $274 million in 1991.
- Bakeware sales have grown 44 percent in the last 5 years, reaching sales of $177 million (wholesale) in 1990.
- Nonstick bakeware accounts for 60 percent of the annual market, almost $100 million in sales.
- Twenty-five percent of U.S. households own Revere stainless steel cookware.

★ COOKWARE

100% American made and owned:

- Visions® 6-piece set, Oven/Microwave
- Corning Ware® USA, 6-piece Trio set
- Corning Ware® USA, 8-piece baking set
- Pyrex® Originals, 4-piece starter set
- Mirro® 7-piece cookware set
- Wear-Ever 7-piece aluminum cookware set
- Regal frying pans (8-inch, 10-inch, 12-inch), Gourmet Pans
- Revere Ware® 7-piece Copper Clad Bottom Set
- Calphalon cookware
- Club Supra 7-piece cookware set
- Romertopf clay cookware set
- All-Clad cookware

American-owned, and over 50% American parts and/or labor:

- Regal 11-inch Griddle
- Regal 16-inch × 10-inch Oblong Griddle
- Innova "The Kitchen Experts," 10-inch fry pan
- Innova "The Kitchen Basics Collection™," 9-piece Stainless Steel Cookware Set
- Regal 8-piece cookware set
- Sears Frying Pans (8-inch, 10-inch, 12-inch)

American-owned, using less than 50% American parts and/or labor:

- Sears 7-piece Stainless Steel Cookware Set
- Newcor Pro-Lum™ Sauté pans (8-inch, 12-inch)
- Cuisinart® Stainless Steel cookware
- Tools of the Trade cookware
- Williams-Sonoma copper cookware
- Williams-Sonoma Grande Cuisine Stainless Steel cookware

Foreign-owned, using American parts and/or labor:

- Farberware® 10-piece Stainless Steel Cookware Set

Foreign-owned, foreign parts and/or labor:

- Le Creuset Cookware   • Circulon™ cookware
- Chantal Cookware   • Meyer Professional 8-piece cookware set

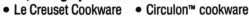

DISHES AND FLATWARE

When you check the label on the only bone china dinnerware made in America, you may be surprised to find that it has a German name! The Pfaltzgraff Company was founded in Pennsylvania in 1811 by German immigrants, and this American company has grown from a modest-size shop producing redware milk pitchers . . . to the country's leading manufacturer of ceramics, featuring more than 55 patterns of casual and formal dinnerware. Today, Pfaltzgraff's 2 million square feet of manufacturing and distributing facilities are staffed by 3,000 men and women.

Another American company with a long-standing tradition of quality is Lenox crystal and china. Started in 1887, this company designed and produced the White House china for President Woodrow Wilson, and they continue to supply presidents with their fine line of crystal and china.

Americans are increasingly interested in sterling silver flatware, and one of the brands they are most interested in is the line made by Oneida Silversmiths. Based in Oneida, New York, where a majority of their products are made, this company recently decided to put their energy into increasing their domestic production instead of creating new products. In the past 3 years they have increased their flatware production by 75 percent, hiring 400 additional people in 1991 to meet the growing demand for their products.

For top-quality American silver, so well-made that it comes with an unconditional warranty, the name to look for is Kirk Stieff. This manufacturer has a reputation for quality that stretches back to the early 1800s, and a current variety of collectibles that ranges from $30 for a letter opener to $15,000 for their 22-inch sterling silver repoussé tray. Now that's what we call a stretch!

American Buying Pattern

■ Americans spend $84 billion each year on housewares.

DISHES

100% American made and owned:

- Corelle® Dinnerware by Corning: "Floral Wisp," "Hummingbird," "Abundance," "Occasions"
- Pfaltzgraff Perennials®: "The Gazebo® Collection," "The Spring-song® Collection," "The Poetry® Collection," "The Tea Rose® Collection"
- Corelle® Living Ware by Corning
- Pfaltzgraff Yorktowne Collection
- Williams-Sonoma Vintage Dinnerware

American-owned, and over 50% American parts and/or labor:

American-owned, using less than 50% American parts and/or labor:

- Newcor Bravo Stoneware
- Williams-Sonoma Blue Denmark Dinnerware
- Williams-Sonoma Green Cabbage Dinnerware
- Newcor Martha Stewart™ Stoneware
- J.C. Penney The Home Collection™

Foreign-owned, using American parts and/or labor

Foreign-owned, foreign parts and/or labor:

- Sango® Stoneware
- Sango® 20-piece collection
- English Ironstone Tableware
- Myott Meakin Earthenware
- Sakura Inc. Vitromaster™

CHINA

100% American made and owned:

- Lenox: "Charlston," "Bellaire," "Chesapeake," "Eclipse," "Republic," "American Home Collection"
- Pfaltzgraff: "Astoria," "Golden Echo," "Blue Organdy," "Madelaine," "Whitney"

American-owned, and over 50% American parts and/or labor

American-owned, using less than 50% American parts and/or labor

Foreign-owned, using American parts and/or labor:

- Royal Doulton USA Inc.
- Royal Worcester Spode Inc.

Foreign-owned, foreign parts and/or labor:

- Wedgwood Ralph Lauren lines: "Imperial Garden," "Empire," "Tartan," "Claire"
- Villeroy and Boch: "Foglia," "Melina"
- Wedgwood: "Countryware," "Oceanside"
- Royal Doulton: "Sherbrooke," "Harlow"
- Mikasa®: "Serenade," "Midnight," "High Spirits"
- Noritake: "Stanford Court," "Pacific Majesty," "Halifax"
- Christian Dior: "Casablanca," "Tabriz," "Renaissance"
- Richard Ginori: "Italian Fruit," "Royal Blue," "Condotti"
- Bernardaud Limoges

FLATWARE

100% American made and owned:

- Oneida Stainless "Fortune"
- Oneida Stainless "St. Leger"
- Oneida Stainless "Woodcrest"
- Oneida Stainless "Cassandra"

American-owned, and over 50% American parts and/or labor

American-owned, using less than 50% American parts and/or labor:

- Gorham "Nouveau" Stainless Steel
- Gorham "Trilogy" Stainless Steel
- Towle "Symphony"
- Dansk "Torun"
- Pfaltzgraff "Yorktowne" 20-piece service
- Williams-Sonoma Flatware "Oxford," "Shell," "Louvre"
- Kornerstones™ 20-piece "Serenade"
- Macy's Cellar Flatware
- Reed & Barton 20-piece Stainless Steel

Foreign-owned, using American parts and/or labor:

- Housecraft Industries

Foreign-owned, foreign parts and/or labor:

- Mikasa 5-piece Stainless Steel "Profile"
- Yamazaki 5-piece Stainless Steel "Fortuny"
- Sasaki "Double Helix"
- Farberware 40-piece set for 8

CABINETS

The biggest ticket in a kitchen remodel is cabinetry. According to the National Kitchen and Bath Association, roughly 37 percent of the remodeling budget is spent here. While you might be tempted by imported hardwoods, the high price tag isn't the only reason to have second thoughts. Honduran mahogany might sound attractive, until you realize that it is being taken from an endangered rain forest.

American cabinet builders are recognized for their innovative craftsmanship. Drop by your local kitchen remodeling store or lumberyard and you'll find dozens of attractive stock designs. We recommend avoiding the European laminates in favor of sturdy units built here. If custom cabinetry is your preference (it represents 78 percent of the market), ask your cabinetmaker to select durable American lumber and avoid imported hardware.

American Buying Pattern

- In the $100 billion home remodeling market, most of the dollars are spent on the kitchen and bath.
- Oak is the best-selling hardwood kitchen cabinet.
- Ready-to-assemble, or RTA, furniture is one of the most popular options that American consumers are choosing. Unfinished cabinets for the average kitchen can be purchased for approximately $1,000.
- Each year over 200 American companies manufacture and sell at least $1 million in kitchen cabinets.

CABINETS

100% American made and owned:

- Ethan Allen "Country French," "Canterbury Oak," "Georgian Court," and "Farmhouse Pine"
- Norcraft "Tudor," "Canterbury," and "Devonshire"
- Mills Pride® "York," "Buckingham," and "Bianco"
- American Woodmark "Continental," "Patriot," and "Affinity"
- Brookhaven® "Winfield," "Somerset"
- Wood-Mode® Design Group 42, Design Group 84
- Fieldstone "Woodridge"
- Merillat® "Meadow Oak"

American-owned, and over 50% American parts and/or labor:

- Les Care® "Mirada"
- Kraft Maid® "Cirrus," "Regency Oak," "Hartland Hickory"

American-owned, using less than 50% American parts and/or labor

Foreign-owned, using American parts and/or labor:

- Quaker Maid® Essence Collection
- Aino Kitchen Cabinets
- Atlantic Cabinet Co.
- Beaver Industries
- Bloch Industries

Foreign-owned, foreign parts and/or labor:

- Smallbone "English Country"
- Poggenpohl
- Allmilmö

FLOOR COVERINGS

From linoleum to plank flooring, it's easy to buy American. Most of the major floor covering lines are made by domestic manufacturers such as Armstrong, a $2.5 billion company with 73 plants in 21 states. While it's possible to buy tiles from Mexico or expensive marble from Italy, there are plenty of American-made alternatives. When it comes to workmanship, appearance and cost, our products are easily number one.

When shopping around, you'll want to consider all your options, such as rubber, ceramic, hardwood, and stone. Each has important advantages. While low-cost solutions may be appealing, keep in mind that higher-priced flooring may be more economical in the long run. Hardwood can be refinished, while vinyl has to be replaced.

American Buying Pattern

- Americans spend $2.9 billion annually on floor coverings.
- The popularity of ceramic tile increased 25 percent in 1991.
- The United States market for ceramic tile was 866 million square feet in 1991, 50 percent of which was manufactured in the U.S.A.
- 56 percent of ceramic tile is applied to floors, 42 percent to walls.
- Would you believe that 5 percent of our nation's kitchen floors are carpeted?

FLOOR COVERINGS

100% American made and owned:

- Armstrong Solarian® vinyl sheet flooring and floor tiles
- Nafco Granite vinyl floor tiles
- Nafco Decorative Vinyl Covering
- Amtico Carefree vinyl floor tile
- Mannington® Gold vinyl sheet flooring
- Mannington® Omnia vinyl sheet flooring
- Congoleum vinyl sheet flooring and floor tile
- Bruce® Solid Oak Parquet wood flooring
- Bruce® Reunion Plank wood flooring
- Hartco Solid Oak Parquet wood flooring
- Anderson Lincoln Plank wood flooring
- American Olean Natura® Designer ceramic tile
- American Olean Subtle Steps™ ceramic tile
- GTE Prominence ceramic tile
- Summitville Imperva ceramic tile

American-owned, and over 50% American parts and/or labor

American-owned, using less than 50% American parts and/or labor:

- American Olean Triad Granite ceramic tile
- Wenczel Reflections ceramic tile

Foreign-owned, using American parts and/or labor:

- Marazzi ceramic tile
- Crossville Cross Colors Ceramic Tile
- International American Ceramics
- Monarch Tile Mfg. Inc.

Foreign-owned, foreign parts and/or labor:

- Domco Vinyl Flooring
- Boen Longstrip Oak wood flooring
- Johnson ceramic tile
- Crossville Mineral Collection ceramic tile
- Crossville Water Series ceramic tile

FOOD

Do you really need us to remind you that American products are almost always your best food value? Here are the facts: American food products are fresher, generally less expensive, and compare favorably to most foreign imports. Our food exports are prized all over the world. The Japanese are paying $10 for that pint of strawberries that cost you a dollar or two. Following are stories of a few homegrown food products that you might want to give a try.

Did you know that most of the imported teas that Americans purchase have spent a year getting here? If you're a tea drinker and like your tea fresh, you should know about American Classic, an orange pekoe tea grown on 127 acres in Wadmalaw Island, South Carolina. Their tea makes it from the field to the grocery store in less than a month. You can reach them at 1–803–559–0383.

The oldest soft drink in America was initially created as a nerve medicine by Dr. Augustus Thompson in 1884. Thousands of people flock to Lisbon Falls, Maine, each year to celebrate Moxie Soda Pop. This American refreshment is made with the root of the yellow gentian plant. Moxie Soda Pop is distributed by Kennebec Fruit Company. Their number is 1–207–353–8173.

With three children to feed and a husband out of work, in 1937 Dona White popped up some popcorn in her basement, put it in brown paper bags and sold it door to door for 10 cents a bag in order to help make ends meet. Her idea grew into the Velvet Creme Popcorn Company, and today they ship their 6.5 gallon cans of popcorn all over the world. To try this kernel of American ingenuity for yourself, call 1–800–552–6708.

From California wine to South Carolina tea, the possibilities are endless. Sour cherries from Michigan, Idaho potatoes, Andersen's Split Pea Soup, Frango Mints, and lobster from Maine are just a few of the American specialties you might want to try. To find the best products, pick up a copy of *Food Finds: America's Best Local Foods and the People Who Produce Them,* written by identical twin sisters Allison and Margaret Engel.

THE LIVING ROOM

The living room, more than any other room in the house, is where we put our finest on display. It's a reflection of our taste and style, always on its best behavior. Just as the furnishings we choose for this room reflect our own personal taste, they can be a reflection of the fine workmanship produced in our own country.

American designs are having a big impact around the world right now, with European manufacturers copying our Shaker, Mission, and Prairie styles in appropriate woods such as oak, maple, and pine. Some people feel that for furniture design inspiration, the center of gravity is shifting from Milan, Italy, to High Point, North Carolina, the furniture capital of the United States. While it's good to know that the rest of the world is looking to us for inspiration, it's even more gratifying to realize that, for the best in price, workmanship, and design, we don't have to look beyond our own shores.

Take an Inventory

Congratulations! You've decided to redecorate or simply replace a table lamp or area rug for the living room. Now is a good time to consider where your present furnishings came from. Are your lamps resting on teak end tables from Southeast Asia . . . are your draperies made of fabric woven in England . . . and that Oriental rug you adore, was it made in the Mideast? Before you shop for another treasure for this special room, take the time to consider all the wonderful home furnishing designs made right here at home.

Don't Be Fooled

As you shop for furniture, have you thought about where—and by whom—the furniture is made? In other chapters, we've shown you that some of the companies you may think of as being American are actually foreign-owned, and their products made outside this country. Fortunately, when you buy furniture from an American manufacturer, you can be reasonably sure that the company is American-owned, and that the goods were made here by American workers using native woods. And you have plenty of choices when it comes to style.

We tend to associate certain styles with particular areas of the globe, but the fact is, you can furnish your living room as tastefully as you wish, in "Scandinavian modern" or "English country," with furniture made right here at home. Take the Italian leather sofa you've been admiring: The leather may well have come from this country (the United States produces some of the finest leather in the world). Why pay for an imported piece when, contrary to what some decorating magazines would have you believe, you can buy comparable (or better) quality at a competitive price, and the leather never had to take an expensive trip abroad?

Comparison Shopping

By buying American rather than imported furnishings for your living room, are you sacrificing anything in the way of style? Quality? Variety? Choice? The answer is a resounding no! In fact, quite the opposite is true: There are almost 2,000 furniture manufacturers in the United States. By buying imported goods, you're bound to pay more than you need to. On the other hand, an imported "bargain" may be no bargain at all—the price is probably as low as it is because underpaid workers (factory workers in Indonesia, where much of our imported furniture comes from, earn about 15 cents an hour) are turning out vast quantities of the item in question on an assembly-line basis, and with very little attention to detail.

A good indicator of the quality of American-made goods is how well they are received abroad. American companies are finding a growing market for their designs in Europe (where American Southwest pieces are especially sought out), in the Middle East (where the most popular fabric choice is patterned or printed velvets), and Japan (where Pennsylvania House finds their very traditional American furniture selling so well that they've recently opened a branch there).

The Payoff

The living room is certainly one room in the house where it should be easy to be a patriotic consumer. The furniture, fabrics, lighting, and floor and wall coverings made in this country are clearly some of the best in the world.

And isn't it gratifying to know that, in an indirect way, by doing your shopping "at home," you're not contributing to the near-imminent demise of the tropical rainforest or the exploitation of underpaid overseas workers, and in a very direct way you're helping to save American jobs.

• If 1 percent of the estimated 94 million American households purchased a new $800 American-made area rug instead of an Oriental import, it could create 18,800 new jobs for American workers.

FURNITURE

When it comes to furniture, there is a long-standing tradition of excellence—both of design and workmanship—in this country. From the spindle-back chairs created by Pilgrim "turners" to the functional simplicity of a Shaker cabinet or a sturdy oak rocker crafted in the Mission style first popular at the turn of this century, Americans have taken full advantage of one of our greatest natural resources.

That tradition is being carried on by companies like New England Woodcraft, located in Forest Dale, Vermont. They make furniture from American cherry and red oak, and have a special concern for the environment. They were one of the first companies to use a non-toxic water-based finish to reduce the emission of volatile organic compounds (VOCs). Their concern extends to their immediate neighbors as well—every bit of sawdust they create is collected and given to local farmers—because the cows love to sleep on it!

Good native American woods include red and white oak, burls, cherry, and pine. Pennsylvania House uses only wood grown in Pennsylvania and New York for their line of traditional furniture. Their story is one of Americans helping Americans through a time of crisis. Started in 1887 by the citizens of Lewisburg, Pennsylvania, between 1912 and 1917 its workers were producing 5,600 chairs per week. The company suffered a series of setbacks in the 1920s and early 1930s, but its carpenters and millworkers believed so strongly in their company that they convinced local businessmen to form a board of directors and invest in the enterprise. Shares were sold at $25 each, in a campaign that used the slogan "Buy a share and put a man to work." This is still a company that takes pride both in producing quality furniture and in the fact that over 95 percent of its goods are produced in this country. The only exception is rattan, which has to be imported. (Rattan is a wood vine that grows only in the jungles of Southeast Asia, Malaysia, Indonesia, and the Philippines.)

A wonderful substitute for traditional wooden furniture is twig furniture, eminently American and loaded with charm and character. This rustic furniture has been appreciated by both backwoodsmen and the giants of industry who liked to "rough it" at their Adirondack camps. For a catalog, contact Daniel Mack Rustic Furnishings, 225 West 106th St., New York, N.Y. 10025.

You may find it very helpful when shopping for furniture to visit a furniture gallery. Many of the major manufacturers, such as The Lane Company, Drexel-Heritage, Pennsylvania House, and Thomasville sell their line from gallery stores. It's all shown in complete room settings with everything from rugs to artwork, so you may get some inspiration on how to mix, match, and accessorize. Ethan Allen, in business since 1932, pioneered the idea of the gallery store. They now have over 300 galleries worldwide, and did $650 million worth of business in 1990.

One type of furniture that has been around since 1927—the recliner—has become a household institution. The first reclining chair was invented by La-Z-Boy founders Edwin Shoemaker and Edward Knabusch, cousins from Monroe, Michigan. It was a wood slat lawn chair. In 1929, a customer suggested that they make an upholstered version. During the Depression the company held on, even though they accepted wheat, coal, and even cows as payment for their chairs. Today, they still make reclining chairs in many styles, and the feature is built into sofas and loveseats, too. They've come a long way from taking payment in farm animals: 1991 sales reached $608 million.

These companies represent just two of the many American furniture manufacturing success stories.

American Buying Pattern

- The first of the "baby boom" generation (those born between 1946 and 1965) will move into their peak earning years—ages 45 to 54—between 1992 and 1995. By 1995, this group will comprise over 31 million consumers (12 percent of the population).
- With personal income growth predicted to rise in the first half of this decade, the compound annual growth rate for household furniture is forecast at 2.7 to 3 percent.
- The market for American furniture exports has grown fastest in Canada, Japan, and Saudi Arabia.
- Sales of recliners account for about 15 percent of the total upholstered furniture market.
- In 1796, George Washington bought 27 Windsor chairs for the portico at Mt. Vernon, at a cost of $1.78 each.

FURNITURE

100% American made and owned:

Sofas/Couches
- Taos Furniture
- The Futon Shop
- Moosehead

End Tables
- New England Woodcraft
- Taos Furniture

Coffee Tables
- Taos Furniture
- Bassett (Cherry)

Upholstery/Slipcovers (fabric)
- AmeriCraft
- Robert Allen (cotton)

American-owned, and over 50% American parts and/or labor:

Sofas/Couches
- Century Furniture
- Pennsylvania House
- Ethan Allen
- Clayton-Marcus
- La-Z-Boy

End Tables
- La Barge

Coffee Tables
- La Barge
- Ethan Allen
- Bassett (other woods)
- Thomasville

Upholstery/Slipcovers (fabric)
- West Point Pepperell
- Robert Allen (depends on material)
- Mastercraft Fabrics
- Belding-Hausman
- Brunschwig & Fils

American-owned, using less than 50% American parts and/or labor

Foreign-owned, using American parts and/or labor:

Sofas/Couches
- Baker

End Tables
- Baker
- Gautier Furniture
- Furniture Americana

Coffee Tables
- Baker

Upholstery/Slipcovers (fabric)
- American Thread Co.
- United Cotton Goods
- Trovira® (Hoechst AG)

Foreign-owned, foreign parts and/or labor:

Sofas/Couches
- Roche-Bobois

Upholstery/Slipcovers (fabric)
- Fame Fabric
- Osborne & Little
- Unikavaer USA

WALLPAPER

In the first half of this century, Appalachian women found an ingenious way of killing at least three birds with one stone: They recycled used materials, insulated, and decorated their simple log homes by papering the interiors with newspapers, magazines, and catalogs. The paste they used was a flour-and-water formula, sometimes laced with red pepper or rat poison to discourage mice from sampling the "wallpaper." Often, sweet anise or arrowroot was added to the mixture—a built-in room freshener.

Nowadays, choosing a wallcovering is a lot more complicated than deciding between the *"Daily Gazette"* and the Sears Roebuck catalog. The choices run the gamut from washable vinyls to printed papers to textiles. And you can choose from among florals, geometric prints, Victorian patterns, and even designs by famous artists such as Matisse and Roy Lichtenstein.

F. Schumacher, known for its extensive line of high-quality wall coverings, prints 95 percent of them in the United States. Among those made entirely in this country are, appropriately, a line of reproductions of wallpaper from colonial Williamsburg.

American Buying Pattern

- On average, wall coverings are changed every five years.

WALLPAPER

100% American made and owned:

- Chapters Wallcoverings
- Hunting Valley Prints
- Village
- Imperial Wallcoverings
- Sanitas

American-owned, and over 50% American parts and/or labor:

- F. Schumacher (Waverly)
- United Wallcoverings
- Gramercy
- York
- Andorer Wallcoverings

American-owned, using less than 50% American parts and/or labor:

- Hampton Wallcoverings
- Palisades Prints
- Boltatex

Foreign-owned, using American parts and/or labor:

- Textile Wallcoverings International

Foreign-owned, foreign parts and/or labor:

- Birge Wallcoverings
- Cherry Hill Studio
- Mohr

WINDOW TREATMENTS

The right window covering can make or break a room. Apparently, Americans are looking to the experts for help in this area. According to a *Better Homes and Gardens* survey, the average interior design studio sells close to $250,000 worth of products annually, and sales of window treatments account for over 40 percent of that figure.

Things seem to be looking up for American makers of decorative fabrics. AmeriCraft, true to their name, makes 100 percent of their line of decorative fabrics in this country. They reported an increase in wholesale earnings of 94 percent from 1991 to 1992, with their fabrics being used not only for draperies, but also by such well-known companies as Ethan Allen, Broyhill, Bassett, and La-Z-Boy.

There should be no problem finding American-made window shades, blinds, and shutters.

American Buying Pattern

- $482 million worth of draperies were sold in the United States in 1991.
- Most sales of draperies are in the made-to-measure area.
- In 1991, sales of pleated shades reached $279 million, vertical blinds $390 million, and mini-blinds $600 million.

WINDOW TREATMENTS

100% American made and owned:

- AmeriCraft
- Kast
- Metalon Drapery Lining
- Milliken Drapery
- Waverly Drapery
- Kirsch Shades
- Joanna Shades

- Bali Blinds
- Superior Fabric Blinds
- Burlington House
- Cameo Curtain
- Home Curtain
- Miller Curtain
- Richloom Fabrics

American-owned, and over 50% American parts and/or labor:

- Country Curtains (Irish Lace, American Cotton)
- Norman's of Salisbury
- Jo-Vin/Quiltco
- Lauverdrape/Home Fashions
- Del Mar Environments Blinds/Shades

American-owned, using less than 50% American parts and/or labor:

- Pier I Import Canvas Blind
- Pier I Import Matchstick Blind
- Kirsch® Mini-Vinyl Blind
- Elizabeth Gray Fabric Pleated Shade
- Jencraft Blind
- Levolor® Blind
- Sears Skyline Vinyl Blind
- Joanna® Mini Vinyl Blind

Foreign-owned, using American parts and/or labor:

- Verosol
- Hunter-Douglas International
- Indoor Window Designs
- Amtex Blinds/Shades
- Koch Julius USA Inc.

Foreign-owned, foreign parts and/or labor:

- Venetianaire Blind

WOOD FLOORING

In that quintessential American tale, Laura Ingalls Wilder described the solid oak floor her "Pa" made for their "little house on the prairie" as smooth and firm and hard, a good floor that would last forever.

The floor is literally the basis of the living room, the setting for your furniture, and there is a lot to be said for choosing wood flooring. Wood is durable, resilient, easy to care for, and actually improves with age. Polished and gleaming, it's the perfect backdrop for colorful area rugs, or the floor itself can be painted or stenciled.

A wood floor is also a sound choice for easy, toxin-free cleaning. Whether painted or finished, all it needs most of the time is a gentle mopping with a small amount of washing soda in a gallon of hot water, and a rinse with clear water.

American Buying Pattern

- Most pre-finished wood floors cost between $5 and $6 per square foot. Double this price, and a professional will install it for you.
- Tongue and groove strip is the best-selling wood flooring in America.

WOOD FLOORING

100% American made and owned:

- Bruce
- Hartco
- Mannington
- North American

American-owned, and over 50% American parts and/or labor

American-owned, using less than 50% American parts and/or labor

Foreign-owned, using American parts and/or labor:

- Coats & Clark
- Arcade Dimensions
- Potsdam Lumber
- Wood Mosaic
- Nooyen Brothers Inc.
- Elof Hansson
- Eaton Provost Ltd.
- Harris-Tarkett

Foreign-owned, foreign parts and/or labor:

- Boen

WALL-TO-WALL CARPET

The choices are almost endless if you opt for wall-to-wall carpeting. There are at least 5,000 different carpets on the market, in more colors and textures than you ever thought existed. Many carpet manufacturers have mills right here in the United States, among them Bigelow, Cabin Crafts, Lee, Masland, and Galaxy.

Wool was at one time the only carpet fiber, and some people claim it is still the best—it resists stains and dirt, is durable, dyes well, and has a springy, luxuriant feel. It is expensive—usually at least $20 to $30 a yard. Most carpeting is now made of either nylon or polyester. Untreated, nylon tends to stain, so it is routinely treated with antistain resins and/or with Scotchgard or Teflon. Polyester is naturally stain-resistant, and also cots less than nylon, but unless the pile is dense and heavy and the yarn tightly twisted, the carpet might tend to mat down under heavy traffic.

So, if you think of your living room primarily as a "showplace," money is no object, and you want the best, opt for wool. But if you have small children who like to drink their grape juice in the living room, choose nylon or polyester.

While it is literally impossible to over-vacuum a carpet, it is possible to over-clean it. The two best methods for general carpet cleaning are *steam* and *dry,* and deciding which is best for your carpet depends on what your carpet is made of, and whether it has been treated to resist stains. Whichever method you choose, you should let a qualified professional do the job. For the occasional accident that needs immediate attention, try Glory®, made in the U.S.A. by S.C. Johnson & Son.

AREA RUGS

Area rugs may best suit your own personal decorating scheme and lifestyle. They come in all shapes and sizes, can be removed for easy cleaning, and you can take them with you when you move.

Buying an area rug that has been made in this country may seem like a bit of a challenge. Orientals are still made mainly in Turkey, Afghanistan, India, Pakistan, China, and Iran by weavers who sit in front of vertical looms tying knots (up to 10,000 a day). As expensive as these rugs are, it's hard to even imagine what they would cost if the people who make them by hand were paid fairly for their considerable labor! In China, they use stitching "guns" to shoot yarn into a backing and produce what look like handwoven hooked rugs. There are acrylic rugs hand-tufted in Thailand, and wool rugs machine-woven in Belgium.

Home decorating magazines and advertising may have you thinking that, while we produce miles and miles of wall-to-wall carpet in this country, you have to look elsewhere for area rugs. Fortunately, this is not the case. American Rug Craftsmen, located in Sugar Valley, Georgia, makes area and scatter rugs in a variety of styles, which include woven rugs, "country" patterns, tufted, and handmade custom border rugs. They are also at work on a line of machine-made "Orientals" to rival those expensive imports. Their rugs can be found at retail outlets across the country, including K mart and Wal-Mart stores.

Braided rugs have been found in American homes since colonial times, though they really became popular in the nineteenth century. A. Leon Capel was the first to manufacture braided yarn rugs. He began the business in 1917. Seventy-five years later, the Capel family is still running the business, and the rugs are made in much the same way. When the braids are plaited, an individual craftsman stitches them together, then puts his or her signature on the finished rug.

American Buying Pattern

- Only 1 percent of wall-to-wall carpeting is now made of wool.
- There are at least 350 carpet mills in the United States.
- The average American home has approximately 70 percent of its flooring area covered in carpet.
- The United States carpet and rug industry is predicted to grow to nearly 1.9 billion square yards annually by 1999.

WALL-TO-WALL CARPETING AND AREA RUGS

100% American made and owned:

WALL-TO-WALL
- Lees Carpet
- Burlington House
- Dupont Stainmaster
- Bentley Mills
- Fabrica
- Karastan®

AREA RUGS
- Sears Best
- Wakefield Mills
- C.S. Brooks
- J.C. Penney By Design™
- Rhody Rug Co.
- Karastan®
- Ash Lawn Capel, Inc.
- American Rug Craftsmen

American-owned, and over 50% American parts and/or labor:

WALL-TO-WALL
- Monsanto Wear Dated
- Davis & Davis

AREA RUGS
- Stark
- Cabin Crafts Custom Rugs
- Davis & Davis

American-owned, using less than 50% American parts and/or labor:

WALL-TO-WALL
- Weave-Tuft Carpet Corp.

AREA RUGS
- F.J. Hakiman, Inc.
- Country Home
- Capel (Orientals)
- Tianjin—Philadelphia Carpets
- Sears Open Home™ Braided

Foreign-owned, using American parts and/or labor:

WALL-TO-WALL
- Dimensions
- Almar Carpets
- Carpets International
- Amtex, Inc.
- Bloomsburg Carpet Industries
- Cumberland Mills

AREA RUGS
- Saxony
- Tapis Oriental, Inc.
- Orian Rugs
- Beaulieu of America, Inc.
- Regal Rugs, Inc.

Foreign-owned, foreign parts and/or labor:

WALL-TO-WALL
- Axminster
- Yale & Francos
  Forman Designs

AREA RUGS
- Pande Cameron
- Shyam Ahuja Ltd.
- Dhurri Rugs
- Hayim Rugs

LIGHTING

Almost any living room can look better and function more efficiently when the lighting is carefully thought out. Depending on how you plan to use the room, you'll probably want some combination of general, task, and accent lighting.

For soft, general lighting, use indirect sources—uplights, recessed fixtures, and wall-washers. This type of lighting is good when you're entertaining a roomful of guests, or just for watching television. Spotlights, floor and table lamps, and downlights can provide just the right illumination for reading. Accent lights can create a focal point for a grouping of furniture, or they can highlight artwork.

Any and all of these types of fixtures are available in hundreds of different styles—from Early American to ultramodern—from American manufacturers. If the sleek, modern look is what you like, don't make the mistake of assuming that you have to buy expensive imported fixtures. Instead, check out George Kovacs Lighting. You'll find comparable style at a better price, and you'll have the added security of knowing that your light fixtures are up to the Underwriters Laboratory (UL) standards required in this country (this can be a problem with some imports).

American Buying Pattern

■ Retailers report that lighting fixtures and portable lamps together account for 35 percent of their accessory sales.

LIGHTING AND LAMPS

100% American made and owned:

LIGHTING
- Basic Concept Ltd.
- Hi Lite
- Keystone
- Wildwood
- Mar-Kel (Ceramics)
- Alsay
- George Kovacs Lighting

LAMPS
- Genie
- House of Troy
- Virginia Metal Crafter
- Hi Lite
- Keystone
- American Lantern

American-owned, and over 50% American parts and/or labor:

LIGHTING
- Koch & Lowy
- Nulco
- Hart Associates
- Murray Feiss
- Lightolier

LAMPS
- Hampstead Lighting
- Amanda Lighting
- Paul Hanson
- Stiffel
- Pier I Import Ceramic
- Quoizel

American-owned, using less than 50% American parts and/or labor:

LIGHTING
- World Imports, Inc.
- Nova
- Progress
- Frederick Raymond

LAMPS
- Frederick Cooper
- Westwood Company
- Fine Art Lamp
- Bauer Lamp Co.

Foreign-owned, using American parts and/or labor:

LIGHTING AND LAMPS
- Carol Lamp & Lighting
- Wonder Corp. of America
- Canrad Hanovia Inc.
- Luxo Lamp Corp.
- North American Philips Corp.

Foreign-owned, foreign parts and/or labor:

LIGHTING AND LAMPS
- F. Fabbian
- Christoph Palme
- Flos
- Arteluce
- Leucos
- B & B Italia
- Artemide, Inc.
- Banci Spa

DECORATIVE TOUCHES

Just what is American decorative art, anyway? A purist might answer that it's Anasazi pottery and Navajo blankets, but that's just the tip of the iceberg. The potters, weavers, silversmiths, and carvers who emigrated to this country may have learned their crafts in their native lands, but they brought their expertise here with them, and began to create wares that were uniquely their own—and uniquely American.

Many of the things that we collect and display solely for the beauty of their form or design were originally made to serve a specific, and often homely, function. There are Appalachian baskets, duck decoys, weather vanes, tramp-art boxes, "schoolgirl" samplers and needlepoint, even spinning wheels and farm implements. And where else in the world has the practical art of quilting been carried to such heights?

Why would anyone want to fill their home with imported plastic gewgaws when there is such an abundance and diversity of American decorative art—interesting objects, with history and purpose. And the tradition lives on. There is a whole new generation of craftspeople, whose creative efforts can be admired—and purchased—at crafts fairs. Fairs are held throughout the year—in Baltimore, Minneapolis, Atlanta, New York, West Springfield, and San Francisco, sponsored by American Craft Enterprises. Its parent organization, the American Craft Council, has information on approximately 2,000 craftspeople on file in its New York City library.

THE
FAMILY ROOM

If the kitchen is the heart of the American home, the family room is its nerve center. It's where we go to entertain, play, and relax. Ever since an American invented the first television, we've sought our entertainment closer and closer to home. Today, the availability of inexpensive rental home videos, large-screen televisions, and video games has given us an infinite ticket to fun.

Just think how many dollars and how many jobs could be kept within our borders if even one television in every home were American-made!

Take an Inventory

As the entertainment hub of the American home, the family room is where our gadgets live, as well as our favorite games and toys. It's a room filled with familiar objects, but a quick look at the origins of that oh-so-familiar television set, VCR, CD player, stereo, and tape deck could be an eye-opener. And while we all know where Nintendos come from, a closer inspection of our dolls, board games, and favorite toys may bring some surprises.

No room better illustrates the plight of our economy than the family room. While many popular products, from the television set to Dolby noise reduction, are American creations, our competitors have effectively seized the market. Fortunately, it's easier than you may think to break the grip of foreign competition.

Don't Be Fooled

When you walked out of the store with that brand-new RCA television set, you probably thought your purchase was as American as a rerun of "Cheers." Likewise, it may not have crossed your mind

67

that your child's well-loved Barbie doll or G.I. Joe Action Figure was manufactured beyond our shores.

The fact that a toy is well-known in the American marketplace does not mean it was made anywhere near our shores. In fact, even some companies with a long tradition of domestic production, such as Fisher-Price, have begun moving production offshore. Examine the label carefully to find out where a product originated.

Comparison Shopping

Nearly every imported item found in a typical family room can easily be replaced by an affordable product made in the United States. While you may spend a little more time shopping for domestic brands, on the positive side, durable, American-made products are highly rated by the experts. There are going to be some times when you may find it costs a few dollars more to purchase an American brand. In many cases, that extra money helps pay for air and water pollution control systems that do not exist in plants operated by foreign competitors.

American manufacturers who make products overseas typically do so to increase profits. Quality is often sacrificed in the process. No one understands this better than foreign buyers who seek out our goods for their outstanding workmanship. (For example, the value of our toy exports jumped 44 percent to $475 million in 1990.) Our toys and games are prized for their creativity; many are considered excellent learning tools. In the following section, we'll show you that home entertainment products, games, and toys made in America are often your best buy.

The Payoff

Most Americans would say their family room is an essential part of their daily activities. It's certainly important enough to the family to be its namesake. Let's extend that concern to the American family in general. When we shop for this room as patriotic consumers, we can use our purchasing power to make a difference in the lives of all Americans.

• If 1,000 American households purchased a $400 American-made pair of speakers, 10 new jobs could be created in our nearly extinct electronics industry.

Home Entertainment Systems

Americans love their electronics. In 1991 we spent $44 billion on home entertainment systems, including televisions, VCRs, stereos, radios, CD players, and tape recorders. While Asian manufacturers dominate the market for these products, American firms are beginning to fight back effectively. New technologies developed here are giving the patriotic consumer more choices. Although many of these products are relatively expensive specialty items, some are likely to move into the mainstream. Equally encouraging, exports of American consumer electronics hit a record high of $1.8 billion in 1990.

TELEVISIONS

If you're looking for an American-made television set, about the closest you can get is a set that is manufactured by an American-*owned* company. Zenith is the last major American-owned television manufacturer on the market. The largest single component in the set, the picture tube, is made in Chicago.

Holding its own against imports, Zenith offers the finest technology and quality on the market today. But it also has to compete in the price category. Zenith found that it can keep production costs down by assembling sets in Mexico with primarily American parts. With sales of $1.3 billion in 1991, it's captured a 13 percent share of the United States television market.

As of July 1993, all new sets will be required to have the technology to display closed captions for the hearing-impaired. Zenith is the only manufacturer with sets containing that technology on the market today.

Asian competitors often try to gain a bigger share of the American market by "dumping" sets on the American market at artificially low prices. Zenith claims that companies in Korea, Singapore, and Canada are trying to evade antidumping duties by assembling sets in Mexico, and then shipping them into our country. While our government has rejected this claim, we can use our purchasing power to reverse the trend.

American Buying Pattern

- Each year, we buy 21 million television sets, worth $6.2 billion.
- Nine and one-half million color television sets were imported in 1990, a 24 percent reduction from 1989. You might be surprised to learn that the leading supplier is Mexico, followed by Malaysia. Japan is the sixth largest importer.
- Roughly 13 percent of televisions are made domestically.
- The "Home Theater" concept, featuring large-screen televisions and high-fidelity stereo surround sound, is an area of the market where enthusiasm is growing.

TELEVISIONS

100% American made and owned

American-owned, and over 50% American parts and/or labor:

- LXI 32-inch
- Zenith 27-inch Stereo, Advanced System 3
- Zenith 27-inch SEq Stereo Surround
- LXI 27-inch
- Emerson® 27-inch MTS/dbx™ Stereo
- Zenith 25-inch Sentry 2 Console
- LXI 19-inch
- Emerson® 19-inch 181 Channel

American-owned, using less than 50% American parts and/or labor:

- Zenith 20-inch Closed Caption
- Zenith 19-inch
- Emerson® 19-inch Color TV and VCR
- Zenith 13-inch
- Emerson® 13-inch 181 Channel

Foreign-owned, using American parts and/or labor:

- Magnavox PIP Total Remote Control
- RCA 35-inch Home Theatre
- RCA 35-inch Colortrak 2000™ Stereo
- Sony 32-inch Trinitron
- Sony 32-inch Trinitron Stereo Monitor/Receiver
- Toshiba 32-inch
- Hitachi 31-inch Stereo
- Sony 29-inch Trinitron Stereo Monitor/Receiver
- Sony 27-inch
- Sony 27-inch Trinitron
- RCA 27-inch Home Theatre
- RCA 27-inch Colortrak 2000
- Mitsubishi 27-inch
- Bang & Olufsen 26-inch Stereo Monitor/Receiver
- RCA 26-inch Console
- Magnavox 25-inch MTS Stereo
- Toshiba 20-inch Stereo, Audio/Video jacks
- Fisher 20-inch Stereo
- LXI 19-inch
- RCA 19-inch

Foreign-owned, foreign parts and/or labor:

- Hitachi 31-inch
- Hitachi 27-inch Stereo Surround Sound
- Mitsubishi 27-inch
- Panasonic 27-inch
- Hitachi 20-inch Surround Sound
- Panasonic 20-inch MTS Stereo
- Sony 20-inch Trinitron
- Mitsubishi 20-inch
- Magnavox 19-inch MTS Stereo
- Magnavox 13-inch Stereo A/V jacks
- RCA 13-inch Colortrak
- Hitachi 13-inch
- Sony 13-inch Trinitron

VCRs

One of the most popular additions to the American family room, the video cassette recorder (VCR), has made the home television competitive with the local movie theater. First introduced to the home consumer market in 1975, video cassette recorders are now in roughly 70 percent of all American households. Would you believe that 90 percent of these VCRs were made abroad? They are.

The first American company to take on the industry's Japanese leaders is Go-Video Inc., which began in 1983 with $60,000 in capital drawn against the personal credit cards of the founders. Initially conceived as a mobile production company (hence the "go" in Go-Video), they soon found that duplication quality was not adequate, and decided to concentrate on developing a dual-deck VCR.

This company now owns the patent on the only dual-deck video cassette recorder on the market. Listed on the American Stock Exchange, sales for this 2-year-old Arizona company took off in September 1991 with the introduction of their "AmeriChrome" circuitry, which can create high-quality copies by bypassing the normal videotaping process.

With consumers purchasing camcorders and VCRs to the tune of 40,000 units per day, you can see why a single unit that can copy and edit a home video with the touch of just one button has become so popular.

American Buying Pattern

- We spend about $2.2 billion to buy 10 million VCRs each year.
- We spent nearly $15 billion to rent prerecorded videos in 1990. Most of what we rented were feature films, but also included were children's shows, music videos, comedy specials, and instructional videos. Some were even on car and home repair.
- Blank videocassette sales accounted for over $900 million in 1990 alone.

VCRs

100% American made and owned

American-owned, and over 50% American parts and/or labor

American-owned, using less than 50% American parts and/or labor:

- Go-Video, Inc.
- LXI VHS HQ Video Head Cleaner
- Emerson® 4-head Remote Control
- J.C. Penney 4-head with titling

Foreign-owned, using American parts and/or labor

Foreign-owned, foreign parts and/or labor:

- Sanyo 4-head Hi Fi
- Sony VCR plus Hi Fi Stereo
- GE 4-head Pro-Fect
- RCA Hi Fi Stereo Home Theatre Series
- Panasonic Omnivision Hi Fi MTS
- Fisher Studio Standard
- Hitachi Auto Head Cleaning VHS
- Sony Stereo Video Cassette Recorder
- Quasar® 2-head Recorder

STEREO SOUND SYSTEMS

As a schoolchild, you probably had to write a report on an American inventor. If you chose to do your report on Thomas A. Edison, you may remember that he invented the first practical phonograph in 1877. In 1956, the Nobel prize in physics went to the three Americans—John Bardeen, Walter Brattain, and William Shockley—who were responsible for the invention of the transistor. In the 1970s, yet another American, an electrical engineer by the name of Thomas Stockham, Jr., created the digital recording process that is the foundation of compact disk technology. These are some of the roots of the American electronic industry that are easy to take for granted when we're busy playing with our modern and all-too-often-imported equipment.

Today, Japan dominates the CD market, supplying more than 5 million units, or more than 80 percent of all imports. Among the top-rated American companies producing compact disk players are McIntosh Laboratories and California Audio Labs.

Although digital recording technology originated in America as a result of developments in the computer industry, no United States firms are producing a digital recorder for consumer use. Because they aren't able to purchase key components, American companies are shut out of this promising market. Many American recording manufacturers are even worried that this technology may lead to wholesale pirating of their products. If you're concerned, write your congressman.

There are some bright spots out there. If you're looking for excellent speakers, consider JBL, a California firm that exports its high-quality products to Europe and Japan. Rockford Corporation in Tempe, Arizona, specializes in car audio components such as amps, speakers, and signal processors. The firm's modular computerized car audio system enjoys a cult following in the 16- to 24-year-old age group "total sound" market. During 1991, this 500-employee firm with manufacturing facilities in Arizona and Grand Rapids, Michigan, did almost $40 million worth of business. Their state-of-the-art sound systems are being exported to Asia, Europe, and South America. This firm's Hafler division is also known for its high-quality tuners, pre-amps, and speakers.

American Buying Pattern

- Americans spend $9.3 billion on audio products, including $3.1 billion on audio systems and components, $1.8 billion on portable tape and CD player equipment, and $311 million on home radios.
- Each year we buy 4.3 million audio systems, 21 million radios, and 10.8 million portable tape recorders, tape players, and CD players.
- Compact disk player sales continue to rise, with Japan supplying over 80 percent of the imports in 1990, which amounted to 5 million units.

STEREO SOUND SYSTEMS

100% American made and owned:

- JBL (L Series, J Series, LX Series, Prose Series)
- JBL Synthesis One Home Theater
- Kinergetics amplifiers and home digital products

American-owned, and over 50% American parts and/or labor:

- Bose Speakers
- KEF Speakers
- Technics Speaker System
- Cerwin Vega! SE Series
- Jensen Speakers
- Advent Speakers
- Dahlquist Speakers
- Infinity Speakers

American-owned, using less than 50% American parts and/or labor:

- LXI Five disk Auto Loading System
- J.C. Penney CD, Dual Cassette Player
- J.C. Penney Tabletop Stereo
- J.C. Penney Tabletop 3-disk CD Player
- Hafler Home Amplifiers, Pre-amps, Tuners
- Adcom Amplifiers, Tuners
- Sony Speakers, Models SS-U21, SS-U511AV, SSU-S21
- Klipsch® Speakers
- Polk Audio Speakers
- Boston Acoustics Speakers
- LXI AM/FM Stereo Cassette Recorder
- JBL HP Series

Foreign-owned, using American parts and/or labor:

- Sharp 150 Watt Stereo System
- McIntosh CD Players, Amplifiers, Pre-amps, Tuners, Receivers
- ADS Speakers
- Kenwood Compact Hi Fi System
- Panasonic Compact Audio System

Foreign-owned, foreign parts and/or labor:

- Magnavox 6-disk Multi Play CD Changer
- Technics CD Changer

(continued)

- Sony CD Changer
- Pioneer Multi Play CD Player
- Denon 20-bit 8-times oversampling CD player
- Magnavox 5-disk CD Changer
- Sony 5-disk CD Changer
- Technics 5-disk CD Changer
- Onkyo 5-disk Accu-pulse
- Sharp 5-disk Rotary CD Player
- Kenwood Receivers
- Sony Receivers
- Pioneer Receivers
- Technics Receivers
- Nacamichi Receivers
- Denon Receivers
- Technics Stereo Double Cassette Deck
- Pioneer Multi-Cassette Changer
- Sony Dual Cassette Tape Deck
- Kenwood Stereo Double Cassette Deck
- Sony DAT Recorder/Player
- Yamaha Speakers
- Sony SS-U31 Speakers
- Pioneer 2-way Bookshelf Speakers
- Sony 20-watt Tabletop Stereo
- Shart 20-watt Component Stereo
- Quasar Dual Cassette Player w/speakers
- Fisher® 110 watts/channel Compact Stereo
- Magnavox Compact Stereo
- Aiwa 30 watts/channel Compact Disk Stereo System
- Denon Elegant Personal Component System
- Bang & Olufsen Designer Bookshelf Stereo System
- JVC Stereo Radio Cassette Recorder
- Fisher® Compact Disk Portable Audio System
- Zenith Compact Disk Radio Cassette Recorder
- RCA Hi Fidelity Compact Disk Player System
- Panasonic Portable Stereo Component System

GAMES AND TOYS

From board games to building blocks, America leads the way when it comes to toys and games. Remember all those long rainy days you spent playing Monopoly as a kid, buying hotels and railroads and property with names like Park Place and Boardwalk? Well, Monopoly is a worldwide phenomenon. The video game was invented here by Atari. The Cabbage Patch generation of dolls all came to life on our shores.

Amazingly, nearly three-quarters of the $10 million spent by Americans for toys and games ends up in the hands of foreign manufacturers. Ninety percent of the $5 billion video game industry belongs to Japan's Nintendo. Executives from many top American firms commute to the Far East to oversee the manufacture of popular stuffed toys, action figures, and fashion dolls in the factories of China, Hong Kong, South Korea, and Taiwan. There are alternatives. We're glad to say that there are plenty of terrific toys to choose from that are 100 percent American born and bred.

Games

If you want to buy an American-made game, board games are a pretty safe bet, since most of them are designed and manufactured entirely in the United States.

Every American household should have a Scrabble game, the crossword board game that sells more than two million copies annually in adult and junior versions. It's even available in Hebrew, French, German, Russian, Italian, Spanish, and Braille.

Scrabble is manufactured by the number one game company in the world, Milton Bradley, which is a division of Hasbro. This American manufacturer has been in business since 1860, and is currently operating its own printing and plastic mold facilities in East Longmeadow, Massachusetts. Many of its products are 100 percent made in America, including The Game Of Life, Twister, Original Memory and, yes . . . Scrabble. One of its more popular recent market entries, Scattergories, contains just one element that is not created domestically: the die.

If you want something a bit different, look around your community and you're likely to find many cottage industries creating imaginative toys and games. Your local parenting paper is a good resource.

Another good place to shop is the Lakeshore Curriculum Materials catalog, which features a wide variety of learning games made in our country. You can reach them at 1–510–483–9750.

When it comes to computer games, why not opt for American-made best-sellers like Sim City or Sim Ant from Maxis. We're also high on the American-made "Where In The World Is Carmen San-diego?" from Broderbund. So, too, we might add, are foreign buyers, who have become addicted to this brilliant creation.

American Buying Pattern:

- Last year, virtually all of our computer games were imported.
- China produces over 20 percent of all of our game and toy imports.

BOARD AND VIDEO GAMES

100% American made and owned:

- Battleship®
- Candyland®
- Bingo®
- Chutes & Ladders®
- Checkers® (Milton Bradley)
- Guess Who?®
- Original Memory®
- May I? Memory®
- Monopoly® Junior
- Twister®
- Perfection®
- Scrabble®
- Jenga®
- Real People®
- Scattergories®
- Life®
- Captain Planet and The Planeteers™
- Where's Waldo?™
- "Where in the World Is Carmen Sandiego?" by Broderbund
- "Sim Ant" and "Sim City" by Maxis

American-owned, and over 50% American parts and/or labor:

- Batman® Returns
- Clue®
- Boggle®
- Commotion™
- Taboo®
- Trouble®
- Monopoly®
- Risk®
- Trump the Game™
- Yahtzee®
- Deluxe UNO®
- Outburst®
- Pictionary®
- Trivial Pursuit®

American-owned, using less than 50% American parts and/or labor:

- Boggle® Travel Game
- Sorry® Travel Game
- Mattel® Wheel of Fortune
- Shift Tac Toe®
- Perfection® Travel
- Atari Video Games

Foreign-owned, using American parts and/or labor

Foreign-owned, foreign parts and/or labor:

- Sega Video Games
- Sega Genesis®
- Nintendo® Video Games
- Super Nintendo®
- Game Boy®
- Turbo Grafx™

Toys

If you're shopping for a preschooler, consider some of the durable favorites from Playskool like Busy Box, Busy Gears, and Busy Beads. Little Tikes' Tap-A-Tune and Xylophone will bring music to your ears when you discover they were made here in America, along with most of this company's other toys.

If there's an aspiring architect in your household, you may want to get a set of Lincoln Logs. A traditional favorite, Lincoln Logs were invented in 1916 by John Lloyd Wright, the son of Frank Lloyd Wright. Each year, Playskool sells more than 500,000 of these little prefab homes made from Oregon pine. Abe Lincoln would be proud.

Another safe toy that's also a lot of fun is the Koosh Ball. Created by engineer Scott Stillinger, this bounceless rubber ball has been flying off shelves for five years. It's an American classic enjoyed all over the world.

American Buying Pattern:

- Each year we buy about $4.2 billion games, toys, and dolls.
- Last year, 89 percent of all our dolls were imports.
- China produces almost 50 percent of our doll imports.
- Strong import competition and increased offshore production by American toy makers eliminated 4.5 percent of the industry's domestic work force. Today there are just 27,000 American workers left in this field.

PRESCHOOL TOYS

100% American made and owned:

- Little Tikes® Workshop Measuring Set
- Little Tikes® Carry Along™ Tools
- Little Tikes® Workshop Wrench Set
- Playskool® Cobbler's Bench

(continued)

- Playskool® Busy Box®
- Playskool® Busy Beads®
- Playskool® Busy Gears®
- Fisher-Price® Rock-A-Stack®
- Fisher-Price® Kiddicraft® Mr. Twist Puzzle
- Fisher-Price® Snap-Lock® Beads
- Playskool® Lincoln Logs®
- Koosh® Ball

American-owned, and over 50% American parts and/or labor:

- Fisher-Price® Kiddicraft® Kiddi Car Phone
- Fisher-Price® Play Desk
- Little Tikes® Workshop Tool Pouch

American-owned, using less than 50% American parts and/or labor:

- Playskool® Mr. Potato Head®
- Playskool® Mrs. Potato Head®
- Fisher-Price® Pop-Up Bunny
- Fisher-Price® Kiddicraft® Happy Puppy
- Fisher-Price® Kiddiecraft® Bath Duck
- Fisher-Price® Chatter Telephone
- Fisher-Price® Sand Workshop
- Tyco® Garden 'n' Grow
- Playskool® Busy Soft Vehicles

Foreign-owned, using American parts and/or labor

Foreign-owned, foreign parts and/or labor:

- Tomy® Twirly Whirlies
- Playwell™ Cheery Push-Along Pets
- ELC Pop 'n' Lock Animals
- ELC Touch 'n' Feel Shapes
- Battat Baby® First Shapes
- ELC Pop-Up Farm
- Chicco® Soft Squeak Blocks
- Battat Baby® Pop-Up Music Man
- Shelcore® Musical Phone
- ELC Bathtime Ducks

TOYS

100% American made and owned:

- Hasbro® Super Defender Action Van
- Little Tikes® Cars and Trucks
- Tonka® Cars and Trucks
- Tim Mee Toy Assault Chopper
- G.I. Joe Barracuda™
- G.I. Joe Patriot™
- Playskool® Lincoln Logs®
- TootsieToy® Colored Wood Blocks
- Play-Doh®

American-owned, and over 50% American parts and/or labor:

- G.I. Joe Battle Copter™
- G.I. Joe Air Commandos™
- James Bond, Jr.,™ S.C.U.M. Shark
- Play-Doh® Play Sets

American-owned, using less than 50% American parts and/or labor:

- Galoob® Micro Machines®
- Nylint® Sound Cars and Trucks
- James Bond, Jr.,™ Sports Car
- Remco® Tuff Ones Cars and Trucks
- Matchbox® Cars and Trucks
- Buddy® L Trucks
- G.I. Joe Action Figures
- Disney Action Figures
- Kenner® Action Figures

Foreign-owned, using American parts and/or labor:

- Duplo® Basic Block Set
- Lego® System Blocks
- Parents® Magazine Tracking Tube
- Playmate Toys
- Perego Products
- Combi Industries
- Ektelon Corp.

Foreign-owned, foreign parts and/or labor:

- Urago® Cars
- Revell® Models
- Playmates® Teenage Mutant Ninja Turtles
- Duplo® PlaySet Jungle Friends
- Duplo® PlaySet Pool Pals
- LegoLand® Town System

THE
BEDROOM

The American bedroom is much more than a "bed" room. It's a private retreat, an inner sanctum, a place to "cocoon." We use it for comfort, for dreams and schemes. It's where most of us will spend a third of our lives.

These days, we fill the bedroom with textures and textiles, and have come a long way from the time when sheets were just white. We've organized our closets and color-coordinated the bed ruffle and curtains. Now let's see how much of our dream room can be American-made.

Take an Inventory

Most of us can take pride in the makeup of our bedrooms. Chances are the bed you sleep in, the carpet on the floor, the furniture, towels, and linens were all made in the United States. But as you check closer you may be surprised to find more products from abroad than you first realized. Was that patchwork quilt imported from China . . . that brass headboard . . . Mexico? Did that baby furniture come from Hong Kong?

Don't Be Fooled

Now let's open the closet. Check the labels carefully. Was that jacket brought over from Italy? Is that favorite running suit from China? And what about those running shoes? Were they made in Korea? Also, don't assume that every American design was made domestically. For example, Standard Terry imports Amish- and Mennonite-style quilts from China . . . those Frenchtex terry towels may have been made in Belgium using Egyptian cotton. As you continue your bedroom inventory, be on the lookout for those misleading imports. In this chapter we'll show you how easy it is to buy American-made products for your bedroom. Today is a good time to start working on your patriotic shopping list.

Comparison Shopping

American manufacturers dominate many of the product lines found in your bedroom. For example, most mattresses are made in the United States. Foreign firms find they simply can't compete with our high-quality products. While it is possible to find imported sheets and towels, you'll have a hard time justifying the extra expense. Many bargain sheets brought in from abroad are second-rate products with relatively low thread counts. You should also know that American-made clothes are tinted with colorfast dyes. The same is not always true of imports. And keep in mind that the highest safety standards are typically used by domestic manufacturers of children's bedroom furniture.

The Payoff

Just a little extra effort on your part can ensure that your bedroom is American-made. The same is true of your clothes closet. At every price point, these goods compare favorably with the foreign competition. Why not begin to make the switch right now?

• According to the Crafted With Pride in U.S.A. Council, Inc., if every American would switch a $30 apparel or home furnishing purchase from an import to an American-made product, 100,000 jobs could be saved in this important United States industry.

BEDS AND MATTRESSES

Even though we spend a third of our life in bed, most of us buy this furniture casually. If your mattress sags or has a lumpy feel, you'll want to start looking for a replacement. Since you may easily be sleeping on it for the next ten years, your mattress should be purchased with great care. Among the excellent American-made brands worth considering are Simmons, Sealy (formerly The Ohio Mattress Company), Serta, Restonic, and Stearns and Foster. Sealy Mattress of Northern California, Inc., a different Sealy company, is also American-made but not American-owned.

As an alternative to innerspring mattress sets, you may want to consider a foam mattress. Made from latex, molded rubber, or polyurethane foam, these units should have a foam density of at least two pounds per cubic foot. In general, the higher the foam density, the better. Both Sealy and Sears make first-rate foam mattresses here in America.

One other possibility worth considering is a futon. Like the old-fashioned Murphy bed, this unit serves as a bed by night and folds up by day. It can also double as a couch. While the design is Japanese, many American companies, such as Shinera, create beautiful futons made with colorful, natural-fiber covers. High-end futons often come with a chair or sofa frame.

Finally, you may want to consider that well-known American invention, the water bed. Invented in 1968 by San Francisco State graduate student Charles Hall, this is the bed for people who want to sleep on a liquid shock absorber. American companies like Wavecrest, Liberty, and Kuss offer these affordable units for as little as $130.

American Buying Pattern

- Latest figures indicate that there was a 1.5 percent drop in unit bedding sales for 1991.
- On average, the price of a queen mattress set will run between $400 and $600.
- The International Sleep Products Association predicts a 6.4 percent dollar growth for 1993.

BEDS AND MATTRESSES

100% American made and owned:

- Moosehead Beds
- New England Woodcraft
- Cochran Beds
- The Futon Shop
- Taos Furniture
- Serta Mattress
- Restonic Mattress
- Sealy (formerly The Ohio Mattress Co.)
- Stearns & Foster Mattress
- Ethan Allen (cherry)
- Bassett (cherry)
- Simmons Mattress

American-owned, and over 50% American parts and/or labor:

- Baldwin Brass
- Leggitt & Platt "Berkshire"
- Thomasville
- Henredon
- Drexel-Heritage

American-owned, using less than 50% American parts and/or labor:

- Pier I Imports Wicker
- Bielecky Brothers, Inc.

Foreign-owned, using American parts and/or labor:

- Baker
- Brianza Furniture International
- Natuzzi Americas, Inc.
- Sealy Mattress of Northern California, Inc.
- Nachman Corp
- Castelli

Foreign-owned, foreign parts and/or labor:

- GuangDong Arts and Crafts
- A.L.F. Uno Spa Beds
- Arflex Beds
- B & B Italia Beds
- Columbo Mobili SNC Beds
- Colcones Rosen Mattress
- Conran Stores

DRESSERS, SIDE TABLES, AND BABY FURNITURE

There are hundreds of American companies creating fine bedroom furniture. From traditional cherry armoires made by the Lane Company in Virginia to side tables from the John Widdicomb Company in Michigan, you'll find it easy to locate first-rate bedroom furniture. Grange Furniture in New York makes a beautiful cherry sleigh bed. For a handsome lamp table, consider Jeffco, also in New York. In addition to these specialty companies, also consider such well-known brand names as Thomasville, Pennsylvania House, and Ethan Allen.

When shopping for a crib you'll find a wide variety of choices, with prices ranging from a low of $100 to more than $800. While units may appear comparable, a closer look may reveal significant differences in construction. For example, the Childcraft Crib 'N' Bed is both attractive and functional. As your child grows, the crib can be transformed into a bed, complete with a storage unit. Simmons is another American company that also makes first-rate cribs. No matter which unit you choose, be sure to add padding to avoid accidental bumps.

One of the more popular American-made high chairs is created in Hudson, Ohio, by Little Tikes. For information on a dealer near you call 1–800–321–0183.

American Buying Pattern

- Industry experts predict consumers will spend almost $34 billion on furniture and bedding in 1992.
- Last year the United States imported $1.1 billion worth of furniture from Europe. Italy is the leading European furniture exporter to the United States, with sales of $494 million in 1991.
- Taiwan, the leading seller of furniture and related components to the United States, shipped $900 million worth of furniture in 1991.

DRESSERS, SIDE TABLES, AND BABY FURNITURE

100% American made and owned:

- Ethan Allen (cherry)
- New England Woodcraft
- Taos Furniture
- Bassett (cherry)
- Henredon
- Moosehead Furniture
- Lane
- Pennsylvania House

BABY FURNITURE

- Nuline/Gerry
- USA Baby
- LEA Industries
- Lullabye
- Simmons
- Childcraft
- Tubbs
- Lexington

American-owned, and over 50% American parts and/or labor:

- Henredon
- Ethan Allen (other woods)
- Drexel Heritage
- Bassett
- Thomasville
- Hickory Craft
- Domain Stores
- Lane
- Pennsylvania House

BABY FURNITURE

- Childcraft (some styles)
- Little Tikes

American-owned, using less than 50% American parts and/or labor:

- Domain Stores (antique reproductions)
- Pier I Import Wicker
BABY FURNITURE
- Cosco

Foreign-owned, using American parts and/or labor:

- Castelli
- Universal Bedroom Furniture
- Conran Stores
- Baker Furniture
- Lehigh Furniture
- Lasalle-Deitch Co.
BABY FURNITURE
- European Furniture Industries
- Evenflo Juvenile Furniture Co.

Foreign-owned, foreign parts and/or labor:

- Conran Stores
- Arflex
- B & B Italia Spa
- Driade Spa
- Scandinavian Design
- Silik Spa
BABY FURNITURE
- Ragazzi
- Morigeau
- Baronet
- C & T International

SHEETS AND BEDDING

With dozens of American name brands to choose from, it's easy to be a patriotic consumer when you shop for sheets and bedding. Big players like Springs (Springmaid, Supercale, and Wamsutta), Fieldcrest Cannon, Burlington, J.P. Stevens, and Dan River make it easy to find the perfect set.

You might want to begin by browsing through interior design magazines to look for combinations that will brighten up your bedroom. In addition to color schemes, you will also want to give some thought to fabric choices. All-cotton fabrics, preferred by environmentalists, are better for hot climates. One popular line of all-cotton sheets is Lady Pepperell, offered by West Point Pepperell. Or you may want to consider cotton/polyester blends, which are more wrinkle-resistant and tend to wear better.

When you're shopping for sheet/pillowcase sets, take a look at the thread-count listing, which shows the number of threads in each square inch of fabric. Sheets with a 200 or greater thread count are top of the line. If the count exceeds 180, you're buying a "better" sheet. The coarsest sheets have a thread count of 160 or less.

While most of us buy sheets and bedding at department stores, bed and bath superstores, or the discount chains, you may also want to consider mail-order outlets specializing in American-made products, such as Land's End (1–800–356–4444), Ezra Cohen (1–212–925–7800), Eldridge Textile (1–212–925–1523), or Palmetto Linen Company (1–800–833–3506).

When you're shopping for pillows, keep in mind that most down used in pillows is imported. In addition, you may want to consider purchasing a specialized pillow designed to alleviate neck or back pain. Among the domestic models are the Natural Custom Counter Pillow from SelfCare catalog (1–800–345–3371), the Makura Miracle Pillow (1–800–777–5264), and the Wal-Pil-O (1–213–649–1807).

If you're looking for a comforter, consider a company like Monticello, which makes a wide variety of sets complete with matching throw pillows. They are marketed under names like Living Legacy, Phoenix, Bel Chateau and, for children, Varoom. Also be sure to check craft shops for quilts created by local artisans.

American Buying Pattern

- American sheet manufacturers shipped more than $1 billion in 1991.
- Americans prefer patterned bed linens to white or solid colors, 2 to 1.
- The total sheet shipment for 1991 was more than 168 million.
- In 1991, imports of sheets and pillowcases were almost 4 million dozen, or 12.9 percent of total apparel sales.

SHEETS AND BEDDING

100% American made and owned:

- Martex® Combed Cotton Sheets
- Wamsutta® Supercale Plus® Sheets
- Morgan Taylor® Cotton Blend Sheets
- Collier Campbell® Cotton Blend Sheets
- Springmaid® Combed Cotton Sheets
- Ralph Lauren "Polo" Collection Sheets
- J.P. Stevens Utica® Sheets
- J.C. Penney "Home Collection" Cotton Blend Sheets
- Dan River Comforter Set
- Wamsutta® Supercale Plus® Comforter
- Home Design® Cotton Blanket
- Fieldcrest® Pima Cotton Blanket
- Fieldcrest® Wool Blanket
- Eileen West™ Combed Cotton Sheets
- Fieldcrest® Waverly® Comforter
- Martex® Cotton Thermal Blanket
- J.C. Penney Acrylic Thermal Blanket
- Utica® Palentino Comforter Set
- Jennifer Moore Comforter Set
- Springmaid® Comforter Set
- Morgan Taylor® Comforter Set
- Macy's The Down Pillow™
- Macy's The Killington Pillow™
- Fieldcrest® Touch of Class® Fiber Pillow
- Bibb Sheets
- Carousel Sheets
- West Point Pepperell
- Heirloom Blankets
- Summer Rest Blankets

American-owned, and over 50% American parts and/or labor:

- Macy's McKinley Goose Down Comforter
- Ralph Lauren Feather and Down Pillow
- Ralph Lauren Fiber Filled Pillow
- Westminster Lace® English Garden Bedding

American-owned, using less than 50% American parts and/or labor:

- Macy's Stratton Comforter
- Arch Heirloom Quilts
- Divatex® Flannel Sheets
- Westminster Lace® Dentelle Bedding
- Westminster Lace® Francesca Bedding
- Pier I Import Bedspreads, Shams, Quilts

Foreign-owned, using American parts and/or labor:

- Kitan® Royal Sateen™ Egyptian Combed Cotton
- Sheridan Pillows
- Sheridan Comforters
- Comfort Pillow and Feather Co.
- Brinkhaus USA Comforters/Pillows
- Herrmann Biederlack Blankets
- Descamps STD Inc. Sheets
- Crawford Manufacturing Co.
- Textiles Del Atlantico Bedspreads

Foreign-owned, foreign parts and/or labor:

- Kitan® Royal Sateen™
- Pombinhos® 100% Cotton Sheets
- Tepi® Blankets
- Sheridan Sheets
- Laura Ashley Mother and Child Sheets and Blankets

TOWELS

The $1.4 billion towel market is dominated by solid colors. But manufacturers know that coordinating stripes and embellishments draws consumers like you into the department store's towel wall, shifting your focus away from pricing and point of origin. Fortunately, all you have to do is take a quick look at the label to make sure you're considering a domestic brand.

Virtually all stores feature an impressive variety of American-made towels. Among the best-known companies are Fieldcrest, Beacon Looms, and Dundee Mills.

American Buying Pattern

- Roughly 78 percent of all bath towels sold are solids.
- About 45 percent of all towels are purchased from mass merchandisers. About 25 percent are bought at department stores.
- American towel manufacturers reported retail sales of $1.39 billion in 1991.
- Retail bath rug sales total about $455 million.

TOWELS

100% American made and owned:

- Jessica McClintock® "Brocade"
- Fieldcrest® "Royal Velvet" 100% Cotton
- Cannon Upbeat Solids and Stripes
- Charter Club 100% Cotton
- J.P. Stevens "UltraCheck" 100% Cotton
- Springmaid® "Bill Blass Design"
- J.C. Penney By Design™ Cotton
- West Point Pepperell
- Carousel
- Design, Ltd.
- Bibb
- Thomston

American-owned, and over 50% American parts and/or labor

American-owned, using less than 50% American parts and/or labor

Foreign-owned, using American parts and/or labor:

- Crawford Mfg. Co.
- Descamps STD Inc.

Foreign-owned, foreign parts and/or labor:

- Sheridan Towels

CLOTHING AND SHOES

Dozens of first-rate domestic firms make apparel in all price categories. In fact, you'd be hard-pressed to think of an apparel category that is not well-represented by manufacturers found within our own boundaries. The American consumer knows that clothing manufacturerd in the United States is going to be a good value. Today, 85 percent of all consumers who stop to look at country-of-origin labels purchase domestic goods. A number of major retailers, such as Wal-Mart, K mart, and Sears have even begun Made In U.S.A. promotions in their clothing departments.

No matter where you shop, you'll likely find clerks happy to recommend apparel made in the U.S.A. When looking through the clothes racks yourself, you may notice some garments carrying a hangtag marked with the "Crafted with Pride in U.S.A." logo. This tag offers a quick way for you to tell that an item is American-made. Any garment bearing this tag must be 100 percent American cut and sewn and manufactured from domestically produced materials. The tags are the result of a labeling campaign by the Crafted with Pride in U.S.A. Council, Inc., an organization whose members come from the United States fiber, textile, and apparel industries. One of their goals is to promote consumer awareness and to get the word out about the quality and value of American-made garments. For more information, you can contact them at 1–212–819–4397 or write the Crafted with Pride in U.S.A. Council, 1045 Avenue of the Americas, New York, N.Y. 10018.

American manufacturers have pioneered many leading fabrics. A good example is Visa by Milliken, which releases most oily stains without pretreatment. You'll also find that odors wash right out of this freedom fabric. In addition, American fabrics typically have the best color retention and far outlast cheaper foreign imports. Equally important, Visa and similar permapress fabrics created in the United States have excellent wrinkle resistance, which means they don't need ironing.

When it comes to men's clothing, you can find everything from Hanes socks to Stetson hats made in the U.S.A. Calvin Klein jeans, Hathaway, L.L. Bean, and Land's End shirts, as well as Kuppenheimer suits, are also popular. Pendleton Mills makes a nice line of woolen jackets for men. Hart Schaffner and Marx clothing are another good example of men's fashions available from American companies. And you can dress American down to your shorts. Briefs were pioneered by Jockey in 1934.

Women can choose American-made clothes from dozens of top companies. From Forecaster coats to Jones New York suits, the choices are numerous. L.L. Bean, Land's End, and Calvin Klein all offer attractive women's sweaters and separates. Jeans from Guess and Calvin Klein are also made in the U.S.A.

Every parent knows that Oshkosh and Health-tex make excellent children's clothing. Other good choices include Lee jeans, the popular Gotcha line, and products made by Pacific Coast Highway. In addition to retail outlets, many mail-order firms specialize in domestic children's clothes. They include Land's End (1–800–356–4444), Children's Wear Digest (1–800–433–1895), and Olsen's Mill Direct, a major supplier of the Oshkosh line. For traditional clothes, try The Children's Shop (1–800–426–8716). Biobottoms (1–707–778–7945), Garnet Hill (1–800–622–6216), and Maggie Moore (1–212–543–3434) all specialize in natural-fiber kids' clothing.

For Afrocentric products, try Spike's Joint, a fashion chain founded by film director Spike Lee.

Although American companies dominate the domestic shoe market, many firms import their product from abroad. Among the manufacturers that do produce shoes domestically are New Balance, a company known for offering hard-to-fit widths. Their excellent shock absorption helps runners avoid injury.

Another domestic success story is Margot Fraser's Birkenstock Footprint Sandals, which sells more than 1 million pairs of shoes and clogs annually. Although they are made in Germany, this company distributes products through major shoe outlets across the country. And they now offer a model designed for the professional person to go with business attire. For something a little dressier, and made in the U.S.A., consider loafers from Sebago or Bass and the comfortable Dexter and Timberland lines.

Many domestic companies make quality women's shoes, including Selby and Capezio. Pickings are slimmer in the children's department. Except for Vans, a popular line of tennis shoes fashioned from canvas, you'll have difficulty finding many American brands. Among the exceptions is Converse's domestically made Chuck Taylor shoe.

American Buying Pattern

- Americans spend $210 billion annually on clothing and shoes.
- Men's outerwear is the most popular export category.
- Exports of apparel and fabricated textiles accounted for 6 percent of product shipments in 1991.
- During the past few years, American manufacturers of childrens' clothing report increased shipments. This has been attributed to the trend of women having children later in life, and having more money to spend on their children's clothes.
- America's apparel and fabricated textile industry is operating at 72 percent of capacity.

The apparel industry changes styles and production locales more often than most other industries. Instead of our usual product key, we have listed a representative sampling of companies who have sourced and manufactured at least 75 percent of their 1992 clothing lines in the U.S.A. A more complete Resource List is available through the Crafted With Pride in U.S.A. Council, Inc.

WOMEN'S DRESSES

ACT I	Gillian
After 5	Jandi Classics
Allison Collectibles	Jessica Howard
Berstein & Sons	Jones New York
Betsy's Things	Jordan Fashions
Brenner, Inc.	Land & Sea
Byer of California	Langtry, Ltd.
Carole Little	Leslie Fay, Inc.
Castleberry	Lisa Deb
Chetta B. Inc.	L. Rothchild
Country Miss	Nat Kaplan
Eklektic	Norma Kamali
Evan Picone	Paul Stanley, Ltd.
Expo	Personal Petites

R & M Kaufman
Rhoda Lee
Scott McClintock
Selador Missy SW

Sportwirl
Stuart Allen
Tribute Dress Company
Victor Costa

WOMEN'S SPORTSWEAR
Action West
Aileen, Inc.
Bayley Sportswear
Cal Cru Co., Inc.
Catalina
Cherokee
Cole of California
David Brooks
Devon
Ease
Evan Picone
EZ Sportswear
Gotcha Covered
Guess
Hartmarx
Highlander
Impressions
Izod

Jantzen
J H Collectibles
Joyce Sportswear
Karen Kane
Koret of California
LA Directions
Larry Levine
Lloyd Sportswear
London Fog
Mary Anne Restivo
Mona Lee
Palm Beach (Evan Picone)
Pendleton
Requirements
Richard Lazarus
Santa Fe
Skyline Northwest Corp.
Unity Knitting Mills

MENSWEAR
After Six
A.H.M. Apparel
Arrow
Bellwether, Inc.
BonHomme Shirtmakers
Calvin Clothing
Christian Dior
Cliftex
Clifton Shirt Co.
Cricketeer

Evan Picone
Garan Inc.
Haggar
Hartmarx
Heralcorp Ind/Knit Stitches
Jaymar-Ruby
Jem Sportswear
Jockey
Joe Boxer
John Alexander

Johnstown Knitting Mills
Kromer Cap Co.
Lanier Clothes
Leath McCarthy & Maynard
Mark Alexander
Nino Cerutti
Pajama Craft, Inc.
Palm Beach
Pannil Knitting Co.
Paul Samuel
Puritan

Ratner Corp (MW)
Skyline Northwest Corp.
Snake Creek Mfg. Co.
Stanley Blacker
Stock Hill/Bert Newman
The Steubwurtzel Co.
Turnburry
20/20 Sport Inc.
Warren Sewell Clothing
West Knitting Mills

ATHLETICWEAR

Artex Mfg. Co., Inc.
Champion Products, Inc.
Felco Athletic Wear Co., Inc.
Holloway Sportswear

Moving Comfort
Russell Athletic
Velva Sheen Mfg., Co.

CHILDREN'S WEAR

Absorba, Inc.
Adorable Children
Allison Mfg.
American Argo Corp.
Andover
Ashland Knitting
Baby Boxers, Inc.
Back 2
Baylis Company
Bits & Pieces
Blue Bird Knitwear
Bonnie Jean
Bullfrog Knits
BUM Equipment
Buster Brown
California
Calvin Clothing

Catalina
Carter
Champion
Cherokee
Chow Baby
CR Gibson
Denton Mills
Dundee Mills
Eastern Sportswear
Embassy
Farah
Fisher-Price
Frog Pond/Kids Inc.
Gerber Products
Go Baby Go Mfg.
Grace Company
Guess

Hanes Knitwear
Happy People
H.D. Lee Company
Health-tex
Her Majesty
HIP Industries
Horizon Design
Hush Puppies Boyswear
Hush Puppies Girlswear
Jandi Classics
Jet Set
J.G. Hook
Jockey for Boys
Johnstown Knitting Mills
Just Bottoms & Tops
Kids Club, Inc.
Knit Mates
Land & Sea
Levi
Little Lady
Made in America Apparel
Monday's Child
My Michelle

Nazareth/Century Mills
Nicole
Nike
The Obion Company
O.P. (Girls 7–14)
Oshkosh
Pacific Coast Highway
Pilgrim Sportswear
Polo
Rare Editions
Reed Mfg. Co.
Roanna Togs
Snoopy
Sugar Togs
TFW-Kidz
20/20 Sport Inc.
UFO Contemporary, Inc.
Union Bay Sportswear
U.S. Apparel
The William Carter Co.
Wormser Co.
Wundies Industries
Young Rascals

SHOES— WOMEN AND MEN

100% American made and owned:

- Bass Weejuns Loafers
- Cole-Hahn (men)
- Dexter Shoes
- Easy Spirit® Dress Shoes and Walking Shoes
- Minnetonka Moccasins (women)
- Sebago Campsides (women)
- Naturalizer® Dress Shoes (women)
- Naturalizer® Natural Sport (women)
- Sebago Docksides (men)
- Timberland Loafers (men)
- Bass Suede Bucks (men)
- Converse All Stars
- Nike Aqua Gear
- Saucony® Jazz 3000
- Teva® Sandals
- Florsheim (men's dress shoes)
- Walk-Over
- Allen Edmonds

American-owned, and over 50% American parts and/or labor:

- Cobbie® Dress Shoes
- Naturalizer® Dress Shoes
- Vans Sneakers (men)
- Lifestride® (women)

American-owned, using less than 50% American parts and/or labor:

- Bass Sneakers
- Timberland Sandals and Boots
- Rockport, DresSports, and RocSports
- Keds® Sneakers
- Easy Spirit® Sneakers
- H H Brown

(continued)

- Nine West (women)
- Evan-Picone Sport (women)
- Esprit (women)
- Sam & Libby (women)
- Bandolino® (women)
- Liz Claiborne (women)
- Pappagallo (women)
- Amalfi (women)
- Florsheim (most styles)
- Converse (most styles)
- Thornton Bay (men)
- Alfani (men)
- Sperry Top Sider (men)
- Reebok Aerostar Trainer
- Nike Air

Foreign-owned, using American parts and/or labor:

- Hanover (men)
- Bostonian Crown Windsor (men)
- Endicott Johnson Corp(men)
- Aviva Group
- Kaufman Footwear
- Grace Shoe Mfg. (women)
- Trent Shoes
- Frye Boots
- Georgia Durango Boots

Foreign-owned, foreign parts and/or labor:

- Clarks Sandals
- Rieker (women)
- Sesto Meucci (women)
- Salvatore Ferragamo (women)
- Via Spiga (women)
- Unisa® (women)
- Enzo® (women)
- Bostonian Loafers (men)
- Generra Collection (men)
- Georgio Brutini® (men)
- Asics®
- Fila
- Tretorn
- Diadora
- Bally® (men)

SHOES—KIDS

100% American made and owned:

- Stride Rite®
- Baby Deer®
- Nickelodeon®
- Toddler University
- Converse Sneakers
- New Balance
- Champion
- Carpenter Self-Starters®
- Kepner-Scot
- Willits
- Vans

American-owned, and over 50% American parts and/or labor:

- Buster Brown
- Stride Rite®

American-owned, using less than 50% American parts and/or labor:

- Nike
- Reebok
- L.A. Gear
- Keds
- Buster Brown® Wildcats
- Stride Rite®
- Sam & Libby

Foreign-owned, using American parts and/or labor:

- Trimfoot

Foreign-owned, foreign parts and/or labor:

- Adidas
- K-Swiss
- Osaga
- Diadora

THE BATH

Our American "rest" room has come a long way. In one short century, we've gone from purely functional facilities to designer decorated bathrooms in the latest styles and colors. Some bathrooms are even equipped with luxury touches such as a hot tub, shower massage, whirlpool, or sauna. Americans are spending a lot of money on the bathroom these days, and it's a great room to equip with the finest in domestic products.

Take an Inventory

From the birth of the terry towel to the golden era of whirlpool pioneer Candido Jacuzzi, the bathroom has been an inspiration to generations of imaginative designers. But did you know it may also be an important component of your mental health? A *Psychology Today* study actually suggests that "too few bathrooms in a home may contribute to family stress."

Look around your bathroom and you'll quickly be struck by the impressive number of "Made in America" labels. Chances are, most of your principal fixtures were manufactured here. Unless you've imported a bidet from France, your toilet was most likely made in the United States. The same is probably true of your shower and tub. That's because efficient American companies dominate the market for bath fixtures, providing top quality at prices few foreign competitors can match.

Only when you get to personal care products are you likely to find foreign companies making significant inroads, particularly among small appliances and toiletries. But even here it's easy to support your fellow Americans by choosing high-quality domestic products. Take our advice and you can easily make sure the content of this room is 100 percent American-made.

Don't Be Fooled

While American firms dominate the market for bathroom fixtures, you could still be duped into buying foreign-made. For example, that friendly-looking Washlet toilet is actually built by Japan's leading toilet company, Toto Ltd. If you're contracting for a bathroom remodel, make sure that your builder specifies 100 percent American-made products. You also need to be alert in the appliance department. Norelco, which markets a popular line of shavers, is often perceived as an American company when, in fact, this Dutch-based manufacturer imports its shavers from Asia. And Salton's "Snoopy's Hairdryer" comes from China. Be sure to take a close look at the label before making your purchase.

Comparison Shopping

Why care if bathroom fixtures or personal care products were made here? To begin with, domestic products are usually your best value. Imports can easily cost twice as much, particularly if they are European. If you do find a foreign-made bargain, there's a chance this product will prove less durable. Safety is another reason to buy domestic. American-made hair dryers now come with a special safety switch that shuts the unit down when it comes in contact with water. And, remember, when it comes to buying spare parts, you'll have a much easier time locating what you need from a domestic manufacturer. It's also good to know that a number of progressive American firms are leading the way by banning animal testing of their toiletries and cosmetics.

The Payoff

Since most of your bathroom is probably already made in America, this room is an easy one for the patriotic consumer. Just be sure to avoid imports at the drug store, the plumbing supply store, and the appliance store.
- If 100,000 Americans were to spend $100 on American-made perfume or cosmetics instead of imported brands, 250 new jobs could be created.
- Experts estimate that 8.2 million electric shavers will be replaced in 1992. If Americans replaced all of them with $35 American-made models, 7,175 new jobs could be created.

TUBS AND FAUCETS

Until the early twentieth century, most bathtubs were white and sat on claw feet. But as the hospital look gave way to more imaginative design, the traditional enamel-covered iron tub was replaced by an array of colorful porcelain models. And as the tub became standard issue in new American homes, manufacturers came up with creative new ways to clean up. The creation of whirlpool devices by American companies like Jacuzzi has transformed the tub into the centerpiece of many bathrooms. (Jacuzzi is now owned by a British company.) A mainstay of the American plumbing industry, the bath has also been a windfall for such home spa manufacturers as Pollenex, Metronic, and Houseworks. For those who demand the very best, there's American Standard's Sensorium Ambiance bathtub, which comes with its own computer and video monitoring system. Another American company, Human Dynamics of Oxford, Mississippi, has created a bathtub that is ideal for the physically challenged. It's just as easy to enter this tub as it is to get into bed.

This restful spot we call the tub is also a boon for the American bubble-bath industry. Dozens of small American companies make bubble bath that competes favorably with European imports.

When running the water for your bubble bath, have you ever stopped to look at your faucet? American faucets are so dependably made, you'll never have reason to consider an import. One of the most popular faucet brands is Delta, made by Masco in Greensburg, Indiana. This firm helped popularize the efficient single-handle kitchen faucet in the fifties. There's a good chance you own one. Firms such as American Standard and Eljer also make faucets in a wide price range. If anything does go wrong, their convenient designs make them easy to repair.

American Buying Pattern

- In 1926, the first colored bathtubs were introduced.
- Almost 10 percent of American households remodel or enlarge the bathroom or kitchen. Over 50 percent of these households "did-it-themselves."
- In 1991, American companies shipped more than 350,000 cast iron enameled bathtubs.

TUBS AND FAUCETS

100% American made and owned:

- American Standard Bathing Pools
- Kohler® Whirlpool Baths
- Passport Ensemble Whirlpools
- Moen® Faucets
- Eljer Faucets
- Eljer Aqualine Faucets
- Price Pfister Faucets
- Peerless Faucets
- Sears Washerless/Two Handle Faucets
- Reid S. Watson & Associates Faucets
- Eljer Acrylic Tubs

American-owned, and over 50% American parts and/or labor:

- Sterling Washerless Bath Faucet
- Sterling Tub/Shower Set
- American Standard Quality Series™

American-owned, using less than 50% American parts and/or labor:

- Sottini Collection by American Standard
- Azimuth Collection by American Standard
- Hastings II Bangno Collection (faucets)
- Norca Faucets

Foreign-owned, using American parts and/or labor:

- Jacuzzi® Whirlpool Baths
- Jacuzzi® Faucets

Foreign-owned, foreign parts and/or labor:

- Dornbracht Faucets
- Harrington Brass Faucets
- Villeroy & Boch
- Jado Faucets
- Hansa
- Gröhe

SINKS

Patriotic consumers need never have a sinking feeling when it comes to buying plumbing fixtures such as sinks. Big domestic manufacturers clearly live up to their reputations. For example, American Standard employs 13,000 Americans in its plumbing products division. This high-quality company, created by the merger of American Radiator and Standard Sanitary in 1929, dominates the bathroom market. American Standard is known for actively supporting volunteer programs in the communities where it operates plants. It also matches employees' charitable donations dollar for dollar.

Another big player is Eljer Industries of Dallas. This 5,000-employee firm, which makes cast-iron fixtures in Ohio and plumbing fittings in Texas, competes effectively with manufacturers in Italy, France, and Germany. Like Kohler, the big Wisconsin-based plumbing manufacturer, Eljer is known for its high-quality sinks.

American Buying Pattern

- American companies shipped more than 623,000 cast iron, enameled sinks in 1991.
- Last year, American companies shipped 3,431,040 metal sinks.
- Latest industry sales figures indicate that Americans prefer countertop drop-in sinks with vanities to the traditional pedestal models.

SINKS

100% American made and owned:

- American Standard (China Pedestal and Countertop)
- Bates & Bates (Brass, Copper, and Natural Stone)
- Kohler®
- Kallista
- Sherl-Wagner
- Eljer (China and Cast Iron sinks)

American-owned, and over 50% American parts and/or labor:

- Sears Victorian Bath Sink
- Sears Hexagon Lavoratory Sink
- Sears Marbella® Sink

American-owned, using less than 50% American parts and/or labor:

- Barkley
- Le Bijou
- Sears China Scallop Sink
- Duravit
- The Imperial Bathroom Company

Foreign-owned, using American parts and/or labor

Foreign-owned, foreign parts and/or labor:

- St. Thomas Collection
- Cesame
- Cerabati
- Sbordoni
- Villeroy & Boch

PERSONAL CARE PRODUCTS

Here's one field where foreign competitors don't have a chance. In fact, it's hard to think of any reason to go offshore to buy shampoo, toothpaste, tampons, cotton balls, cold cream, or any of the hundreds of other products that fall into this category. Operating under strict FDA regulation, these firms make products to standards many overseas firms can't or won't match.

American Buying Pattern

- The American cosmetics industry had 123,000 workers and $42 billion in sales during 1991.
- Soap and detergent sales rose 3.2 percent in 1991, to more than $14 billion.
- More than 90 percent of American women use a deodorant.
- Americans spend about $331.5 million a year on razor blades.
- The electric shaver market is currently worth more than $700 million.
- More than 80 percent of teenage American girls use lipstick.
- According to *Consumer Reports,* an average roll of bathroom tissue contained 400 sheets in 1984. Today, the average number of sheets has dropped to 300.

SOAP

From old standbys like Ivory to specialty products such as Neutrogena, store shelves are dominated by domestic soap brands. One of the biggest players in this field is Procter & Gamble, the Cincinnati-based company that makes such popular brands as Ivory and Camay. Another big player is Colgate-Palmolive and its Irish Spring. You may want to consider a mild glycerine bar soap like Neutrogena (which has traveled in orbit with Sky Lab astronauts!). Or you may prefer the convenience of a liquid soap like Softsoap®.

And then there's Dr. Emanuel Bronner, a third-generation soap maker. After fleeing Germany in the 1930s, he started making peppermint soap in a barrel at his Los Angeles apartment. Today, he ships his popular brand to 3,000 health food stores across America and sends 20,000 pounds of soap a month to Australia. He also ships to Italy and England.

SOAP

100% American made and owned:

- Camay
- Dial
- Irish Spring
- Mountain Fresh®
- Noxema®
- Palmolive Octagon
- Pure & Natural
- Safeguard
- Zest
- Clinique
- Purpose™
- Ivory
- Neutrogena
- Dr. Bronner's Peppermint Soap

American-owned, and over 50% American parts and/or labor:

- Cashmere Bouquet®
- Lubriderm®
- Tone®

American-owned, using less than 50% American parts and/or labor:

- Coast®
- Lava

Foreign-owned, using American parts and/or labor:

- Basis®
- Caress
- Dove
- Jergens®
- Lever 2000
- Lifebuoy
- Lux
- Shield
- Shiesedo
- Yardley of London

Foreign-owned, foreign parts and/or labor:

- Crabtree & Evelyn
- Pears
- Rene Guinot
- Clarins
- Lancôme
- Shiesedo
- Goodbodies®
- Body Shop®

SHAVING CREAM AND RAZORS

What's on the shelf in your medicine cabinet? When it comes to shaving cream, you'll find American brands such as Gillette's Foamy and Pfizer's Barbasol the market leaders. Gillette is also well known for its razors. This company makes a highly regarded cartridge-razor system called Trac II. While men tend to prefer these reusable twin blade shavers, women opt for disposable single blade units such as Flicker, made in the United States by The American Safety Razor Company of Staunton, Virginia. Among other popular American-made razors are Atra Plus, Daisy Plus, and Good News!

You may prefer an electric shaver to razor blades. Here foreign companies compete hard for market share. But as a patriotic consumer, you can still find an American-made brand, such as Remington or Gillette. Men's shavers are made for daily use, while women's models are designed for less frequent shaving. If you're prone to nicks, you may appreciate the convenience of a wet/dry shaver. These shock-proof units, such as the rechargeable Lady Remington Shower Style Wet/Dry shaver, are designed to be used with shaving cream or soap. Currently, there are no wet/dry shavers made in America.

MEN'S COLOGNE, AFTER SHAVE, AND SHAVING CREAM

100% American made and owned:

- Aramis
- Barbasol®
- Colgate
- English Leather
- Gillette Foamy
- Noxema®
- Old Spice

American-owned, and over 50% American parts and/or labor:

- British Sterling
- Canoe (Dana)
- Edge®
- Jovan® Musk
- Old Spice (after shave)
- Schick®
- Soft Sense™
- Stetson (Coty)

American-owned, using less than 50% American parts and/or labor

Foreign-owned, using American parts and/or labor:

- Aqua Velva
- Boss
- Brut
- Chaps (Ralph Lauren)
- Eternity (Calvin Klein)
- Fendi Uomo
- Passion For Men (E. Taylor)
- Pierre Cardin
- Pour Monsieur (Chanel)

Foreign-owned, foreign parts and/or labor:

- Drakkar Noir (Guy Laroche)
- Grey Flanel (Geoffrey Beene)
- Fahrenheit (Dior)
- Sung Homme
- Xeryus (Givency)

MEN'S SHAVERS (BLADE AND ELECTRIC)

100% American made and owned:

- Gillette® Sensor®
- Gillette® Atra Plus®
- Gillette® Good News!® Plus
- Gillette® Good News!® MicroTrac®
- Gillette® Trak II®
- Schick® Super II Twin Blade Cartridges
- Schick® Slim Twin Cartridges
- Remington Micro Screen® Cord (Electric)
- Remington Triple Action® Cord (Electric)

American-owned, and over 50% American parts and/or labor:

- Gillette® Good News!®

American-owned, using less than 50% American parts and/or labor:

- Schick® Tracer™
- Schick® Slim Twin Plus
- Braun Rechargeable (Electric)
- Sears Rotomatic™ Foil Shaver(Electric)
- Remington® Micro Screen Elite™ Cord (Electric)
- Remington® Micro Screen Elite™ Cord/Rechargeable (Electric)
- Remington® Triple Action® (Electric)
- Sears Rotomatic™ Thinline 2000 (Electric)
- Sears Rotomatic™ Wet/Dry Shave (Electric)
- Braun Rechargeable Deluxe

Foreign-owned, using American parts and/or labor:

- Bic® Shaver for Sensitive Skin
- Bic® Shaver for Normal Skin

Foreign-owned, foreign parts and/or labor:

- Wilkinson Sword "Ultra Glide®"
- Norelco Lift & Cut™ Cord/Cordless (Electric)
- Panasonic Smooth Operator® (Electric)
- Norelco Rechargeable (Electric)
- Norelco Cord Shaver (Electric)

WOMEN'S SHAVERS (BLADE AND ELECTRIC)

100% American made and owned:

- Flicker®
- Gillette® Daisy Plus™
- Schick® Personal Touch®
- Lady Remington® Micro Screen® Cord (Electric)
- Lady Remington® Micro Screen® Cordless (Electric)
- Lady Remington® Cordless Rechargeable (Electric)

American-owned, and over 50% American parts and/or labor:

- Gillette® Daisy Slim™

American-owned, using less than 50% American parts and/or labor:

- Lady Remington® Shower Style™ (Electric)

Foreign-owned, using American parts and/or labor:

- Bic® Lady Shaver

Foreign-owned, foreign parts and/or labor:

- Bic® Pastel Shavers
- Norelco Lady Shave Wet/Dry (Electric)
- Panasonic® Ladies Smooth Operator™
- Norelco Splash & Shave

TOOTHBRUSHES
AND TOOTHPASTE

Smile . . . and the toothcare industry smiles with you! Scores of American manufacturers make nylon toothbrushes that dominate the $153-million-a-year toothbrush industry. Among the top brands are Reach from Johnson and Johnson and Plus by Colgate. If you prefer high-tech, consider an electric toothbrush from Interplak. Johnson and Johnson also makes a full line of dental floss.

Choosing an American-made toothpaste is easy. Most major brands like Colgate offer both regular and tartar control. Or you may opt to use a "natural" brand made without artificial sweeteners such as Tom's of Maine.

TOOTHPASTE, TOOTHBRUSHES, AND MOUTHWASH

100% American made and owned:

- Act®
- Colgate (brush)
- Colgate Fluorigard®
- Colgate Tartar Control
- Crest®
- Gleem
- Interplak®
- Oral B® (brush)
- Py-co-pay (brush)
- Reach® Neon (brush)
- Scope
- TEK® (brush)
- Tom's® Natural
- Ultra-brite
- Viadent®

American-owned, and over 50% American parts and/or labor:

- Cepacol®
- Colgate Plus (brush)
- Lavoris
- Listermint®
- Pearl Drops®
- Plax® (mouthwash)
- Reach® Compact Head (brush)
- Rembrandt®
- Zact

American-owned, using less than 50% American parts and/or labor:

- Interplak® (brush)
- Plax® (brush)
- Reach® (brush)

Foreign-owned, using American parts and/or labor:

- Aim
- Aquafresh®
- Close-up®
- Disney Pepsodent® (brush)
- G.U.M. (brush)
- Macleans
- Pepsodent
- Signal

Foreign-owned, foreign parts and/or labor:

- Aquafresh® Flex™ (brush)
- Pepsodent® Professional (brush)

SHAMPOO AND
HAIR CARE PRODUCTS

One of the largest categories in the health and beauty industry is the $1.2 billion shampoo market. This industry, which grows about 5 percent a year, is dominated by American companies Procter & Gamble (Pert) and Gillette (White Rain). The number one seller, Head and Shoulders, includes a dandruff fighter called pyrithone zinc.

While shampoos do a good job treating hair near your scalp, conditioners do a better job on the ends. They also help restore some of the natural oil stripped away by shampoo detergents. Today the $500-million-a-year conditioner industry still has plenty of growth potential. Only 60 percent of American women and 20 percent of American men use conditioners. If you're looking for a conditioner, consider a domestic brand such as Nexxus's Humectress, which can also be used as a hair dressing that moisturizes dry, brittle hair. Nexxus also has an excellent black hair care program. Another company making a popular line of shampoos and conditioners sold primarily in barber shops and hair salons is KMS, based in Redding, California. These environmentally safe hair care products are made without any animal testing. If you're looking for a hair spray, why not go the "green" route and choose one that comes in a pump, rather than an aerosol can? Popular brands include Clairol and Nexxus.

If you're in the market for a blow-dryer, you'll probably want to pick up one of the American models made by companies like Clairol, Windmere, and Vidal Sassoon that come with a diffuser, which allows the user to adjust air flow by turning the unit's grill. This feature provides a gentler airstream that dries without diminishing hair curl. Unfortunately, almost all of these units come from Asia. The same is true of curling irons and hot rollers.

SHAMPOO/HAIR CARE

100% American made and owned:

- Agree®
- Almay
- Breck®
- Head & Shoulders®
- Johnson's Baby Shampoo
- Neutrogena
- Nexxus
- Pantene Progressive Treatment
- Pert Plus®
- Prell
- Selsun Blue®
- Vidal Sasson
- White Rain®
- Redken
- Clinique
- KMS

American-owned, and over 50% American parts and/or labor:

- Clairol
- Clean & Clear
- Finesse®
- Flex
- Paul Mitchell
- Salon Selectives®
- Silkience
- Suave®
- Sukesha
- Systeme Biolage
- Vibrance®

American-owned, using less than 50% American parts and/or labor:

- Pantene® Pro-V

Foreign-owned, using American parts and/or labor:

- Crabtree & Evelyn (Aloe Vera Shampoo)
- Jingles® Healthy Hair
- L'Oreal® Permavive
- Rave®
- Elizabeth Arden Spa®

Foreign-owned, foreign parts and/or labor:

- Crabtree & Evelyn
- Goodbodies®
- Body Shop®

★ HAIR APPLIANCES

100% American made and owned:

- Dazey® Natural Wonder™ Salon Hair Dryer
- Dazey® Natural Wonder™ Hair Dryer model HD31
- Richard Caruso® Molecular Hairsetter

American-owned, and over 50% American parts and/or labor:

- Conair® Thermacell® Cordless Curling Iron/Brush

American-owned, using less than 50% American parts and/or labor:

- Conair® ES1600 Hairdryer
- Salton™ Snoopy's Hairdryer
- Windmere Perfect Pro®
- Salton/Maxim Salon 1250 Professional Hair Dryer
- Vidal Sassoon Professional 1500-Watt Styling Dryer
- Vidal Sassoon Cold Shot Professional 1500-Watt Styling Dryer
- Sears Best Professional Styler Dryer 1600-Watt
- Sears Turbo Mini-Dryer
- Conair® Curl Dazzler™ Plus 1500
- Clairol® EuroStylist 1600
- Salton™ Heatwave™
- Perfect Pro Micro-Mini ⅜-inch
- Conair® Supreme™ Professional ⅜-inch
- Conair® Supreme™ Professional ⅞-inch
- Conair® ¾-inch Full-Size Professional
- Vidal Sassoon Professional Brush Iron ½-inch mini
- Vidal Sassoon Professional Insta-Heat™ Regular ¾-inch
- Windmere® Four-Way Curls®
- Sears Professional Styling Combo

(continued)

- Clairol® Kindness Curl-Technics®
- Clairol® Style Setter®
- Clairol® Curl-Technics®
- Windmere® Hairsetter 21
- Windmere® Gentle Curls® 24

Foreign-owned, using American parts and/or labor

Foreign-owned, foreign parts and/or labor

COSMETICS

When it comes to cosmetics, the key word is choice. Although there are many imports, particularly French products, domestic manufacturers dominate this $42-billion-a-year industry. Frequently, you'll see a woman's name on the product line.

Historically, the cosmetic industry has been a land of opportunity for American women entrepreneurs sich as Elizabeth Arden, Estee Lauder, and Adrien Arpel. Today, Elizabeth Arden is owned by the Anglo/Dutch corporation, Unilever. Other popular American lines include Clinique (only the name is French), and Noxzema Cover Girl. Avon and Mary Kay products are sold by an army of independent distributors, including several who probably live in your own neighborhood.

PERFUME

100% American made and owned:

- Charlie (Revlon)
- Jean Naté (Revlon)
- Jontue (Revlon)
- Beautiful (Estee Lauder)
- Knowing (Estee Lauder)
- White Linen (Estee Lauder)

American-owned, and over 50% American parts and/or labor:

- Tabu (Dana)
- Realities (Liz Clairborne)
- Navy (Cover Girl)
- Society (Burberrys)

American-owned, using less than 50% American parts and/or labor:

- Carolina Herrera

Foreign-owned, using American parts and/or labor:

- Chloe
- Lauren (Ralph Lauren)
- Coco (Chanel)
- Chanel No. 5
- Passion (Elizabeth Taylor)
- White Diamonds (Elizabeth Taylor)

Foreign-owned, foreign parts and/or labor:

- Anais, Anais
- Escada (Margaretha Ley)
- Fendi
- Gardenia (Crabtree & Evelyn)
- L'Air du Temps (Nina Ricci)
- Opium (Yves St. Laurent)
- Oscar de la Renta
- Poison (Dior)
- Rive Gauche (Yves St. Laurent)
- Shalimar (Guerlain)
- Ysatis (Givenchy)

DEODORANT

100% American made and owned:

- Almay
- Ban®
- Dry Idea®
- Lady Speed Stick®
- Lady Mitchum
- Old Spice Stick

- Secret
- Soft & Dry
- Speed Stick®
- Sure
- Tom's®

American-owned, and over 50% American parts and/or labor:

- Arrid®
- Degree
- Dial
- Lady's Choice
- Mitchum®
- Right Guard
- Suave® Super Stick

American-owned, using less than 50% American parts and/or labor:

- Old Spice Anti-Perspirant
- Suave®

Foreign-owned, using American parts and/or labor:

- Brut®
- Faberge Power Stick®
- Lady Power Stick™
- Lady Power Stick™ Roll on
- Babe®
- Pierre Cardin

Foreign-owned, foreign parts and/or labor

COSMETICS

100% American made and owned:

- Almay
- Clarion
- Clinique
- Estee Lauder
- Princess Marcella Borghese
- Cover Girl

American-owned, and over 50% American parts and/or labor:

- Bonne Bell
- Cornsilk
- Max Factor
- Maybelline
- Origins
- Prescriptives
- Revlon

American-owned, using less than 50% American parts and/or labor:

Virtually every American cosmetics company imports some eye, lip, and blush products from Europe and Japan. Here are some examples:

- Estee Lauder
- Max Factor
- Princess Marcella Borghese
- Clinique
- Prescriptives
- Revlon
- Coty
- Almay
- Maybelline

Foreign-owned, using American parts and/or labor:

- Chanel
- Lancôme
- L'Oreal
- Germaine Monteil
- Elizabeth Arden

Foreign-owned, foreign parts and/or labor:

- Carita
- Christian Dior
- Orlane
- Elizabeth Arden (assorted eye/lip/blush)
- Stendhal
- Yves St. Laurent
- L'Oreal
- Lancôme (assorted eye/lip/blush)

PAPER PRODUCTS

You can make an important environmental choice by choosing tampons that come with cardboard rather than plastic applicators. In addition, companies like Kimberly Clark, with their innovative one-ply Kleenex toilet paper, make it easier to help conserve our forests. Equal in softness to two-ply paper, it costs about one-third less.

Domestic makers also dominate the market for first-aid supplies such as Band-Aids from Johnson and Johnson and Curad adhesive bandages.

PAPER PRODUCTS

100% American made and owned:

- Kleenex® Softique®
- Cottonelle
- Charmin®
- Angel Soft®
- ScotTissue®
- Coronet®
- Marcal® Facial Tissue
- Scotties® Facial Tissue
- Today's Choice™ Pads
- Sure & Natural® Pads
- Always Ultra-Plus Pads
- Tampax® Tampons
- Kotex® Maxi-pads
- New Freedom® Thin Maxi
- Johnson & Johnson Band Aids®
- Curad Bandages

American-owned, and over 50% American parts and/or labor:

- Marcal® Sofpac® Bathroom Tissue
- Northern®
- Puffs® Plus
- Marcal® Hankies
- O.B.® Applicator-free Tampon
- Playtex® Portables® Tampon
- New Day's Choice Thin Maxi pad
- Stayfree Super-Maxi

American-owned, using less than 50% American parts and/or labor:

- Stayfree Ultra Plus Maxi pad
- New Freedom® Super Maxi pad

Foreign-owned, using American parts and/or labor

Foreign-owned, foreign parts and/or labor

THE HOME OFFICE

Americans are perennially among the world's hardest workers. It's not enough for us just to work all day; we often bring work home. More than 25 million Americans have taken the extra step of creating a workplace at home—the home office. It can be a small space in the hallway or a room full of complex equipment. Whether we're using the home office as our primary place of business or as a place to finish off the day's overload, Americans are taking advantage of the impressive array of electronic devices available.

Let's get our home offices to really perform—with high-quality, American-made products. We'll be rewarding ourselves and the dedicated manufacturers and workers of this country.

Take an Inventory

Today, American high-tech electronics are second to none. And foreign competitors know it. They license *our* technology in order to compete in world markets.

Such technology used to be as expensive as it was sophisticated. Just a few years ago, only corporate spenders could easily afford personal computers and fax machines. Now they're within the reach of many Americans who want to be productive at home. Take a look around your home office. You're likely to have a surprising amount of equipment. Personal computers, modems, fax machines, and sophisticated telephone equipment now give home office workers the reality of a sophisticated office. You can buy American and be glad you did in your home office.

If you've ever read up on home office equipment in major computer and electronics publications, you've discovered that a great selection of high-quality products are out there. You've also discovered that, especially with high-tech goods, you get more for your money than ever before. Blazing-fast computers, high-speed modems and faxes, telephones that do everything but open the mail—you have lots of choices. But have you discovered which of the companies making the products are *really* American?

Don't Be Fooled

It's easy to think that you're buying American when you see American-sounding names like Sharp, Epson, or Canon. These Japanese companies don't mind that a bit. Even some well-known American companies like IBM and Apple use some percentage of foreign-made components in their computers. Just because the computer, modem, or fax package lists a United States address doesn't mean that the product is made here. Look closely for the small print that often says "Made in Taiwan" (or Korea or Singapore, etc.!).

Comparison Shopping

In spite of foreign competition for your dollars, you can proudly buy American when you equip your home office. American manufacturers turn out innovative products combining high quality and great value. And they back up their products with warranties and service. When it comes to the home office, where quality and dependability are vital to your success, don't be just a price shopper. Be a value shopper and buy American.

The Payoff

From the lowly paper clip to the most sophisticated computer, you can find American choices for every element of your home office. And they're good choices, too, offering great value for your money. By buying American when you stock your home office, you'll be helping to bolster a segment of our economy that employs hundreds of thousands of Americans.

• It is estimated that approximately 3.3 million personal computers will be replaced in 1992. If every $5,000 replacement computer was manufactured in America, 412 new jobs could be created in the computer industry.

COMPUTERS

Today's personal computers are one of the technological marvels of modern times. And they were invented in the United States! From the early tube-powered, room-sized (and relatively slow) monsters of the forties and fifties, computers have rapidly evolved into compact, powerful machines that help take much of the mechanical drudgery out of our business and personal lives. And Americans wrote the book on personal computers: IBM on one side and Apple on the other. These two companies have set the standards for the world when it comes to personal computing.

Personal computers have become a $31.5 billion market just in the United States. More than 28 million American households are expected to include personal computers by the end of 1992. For less than the price of a good sofa, you can own a high-powered personal computer that will significantly speed up tasks such as writing, record keeping, calculations, design, artwork, and much more. Personal computers now can integrate still photos, video, and sound with optional hardware and software. The personal computer is at the heart of most home offices.

Can you make a big mistake when buying a personal computer? Not if you buy quality. Whether it's an IBM or IBM-compatible on one hand, or Apple Macintosh on the other, either of the major operating systems offer you tremendous versatility when it comes to the software available to handle your home office tasks. Just be sure to buy only what you need. While there are some very high-powered personal computers available, their capabilities and price tags may be more than is necessary to handle your home office work. There are good American choices available at a price to fit any budget.

If you're thinking of buying a computer, first decide what kinds of software will best suit your needs, then look for the computer that can utilize this software.

Having said that, let's look at the computer choices available to the patriotic consumer. There are two major computer operating systems in the personal computer market—DOS (for IBM and IBM-compatible computers) and Macintosh (for Apple Computer's line of Macintosh computers). Together, these operating systems account for an estimated 82 percent of personal computers in the home. Both systems were invented in the United States. Until recently, the Macintosh operating system was considered significantly easier to use. Now, Windows software for DOS computers brings a look similar to the Mac to IBM and IBM-compatible computer screens. A software's packaging will tell you which operating system that software will work with, DOS or Macintosh. Some software has versions for each system.

IBM and IBM-Compatible Computers

In the IBM and IBM-compatible world, there are many different brands of computers (generally referred to as PCs) available—IBM has licensed its technology to many manufacturers. If you're looking for quality, it's hard to tell the difference from the outside, as one computer looks much like another. IBM itself uses many foreign components in its computers, though its manufacturing is primarily done in the United States. However, IBM-compatible computers, which work effectively with DOS software, are often made overseas, typically in the Far East. Imports from Taiwan alone accounted for more than $2 billion in American sales in 1991. But are your only choices IBM or foreign IBM-compatible computers? Absolutely not!

You do have a choice in the PC world. Besides IBM, American companies such as Tandy, Dell, and Compaq come highly recommended by computer publications and users. Their quality is excellent and their prices are competitive.

Among American-made IBM-compatibles, one manufacturer, Everex, may be a great choice for your home office. Based in Fremont, California, part of the world-renowned Silicon Valley, bustling with high-tech companies, Everex has grown quickly from its beginnings in 1983 to 1991 sales of more than $425 million, and employs 2,000 Americans. Despite the fact that it is not an American-owned company, Everex manufactures virtually all of its products in the United States, using primarily American-made components. The Everex slogan, "Ever for EXcellence," indicates a serious commitment to quality. It's not just a slogan—Everex computers and computer peripherals have received high marks in computer publications and independent consumer surveys. The Everex spectrum of computers runs from desktop machines to portables to notebook-sized units. If you're looking for an IBM-compatible computer, you'll find some high-quality choices with Everex.

Apple Computer

On the other side of the computer street is Apple Computer, another Silicon Valley success story, known for its Macintosh computers (Mac for short). The Macintosh operating system is noted for its user-friendly graphical user interface (GUI), meaning that you can make things happen by using convenient menus and icons on the computer screen. From humble beginnings in a California garage, the company now has worldwide revenues of $3.8 billion (1990) for its computers, topped only by the mighty IBM.

Apple is an American-owned company and many Apple products are manufactured in the United States. Like many high-tech companies, Apple uses some imported components (particularly in computer printers). Apple computers are extremely well-regarded by consumers and the computer press. Because Apple does not license its operating system technology like IBM, if you want the advantages of the Apple operating system you have to buy their products. However, Apple's prices have dropped significantly and they are very competitive these days, offering you excellent value.

American Buying Pattern

- Every year, we buy more than 10 million personal computers worth $31.5 billion. Of these, an estimated 4 million personal computers worth more than $4.8 billion are used at home. And these figures are growing yearly!
- More than 50 percent of personal computers are purchased from American manufacturers.
- In 1990, roughly 28 percent of all American households owned a personal computer.
- More than $9 billion of American personal computers are exported each year.
- In the United States, Apple sold 618,000 computers in 1990 for American sales of $2.2 billion dollars, second only to IBM.
- Apple computers have an estimated 23 percent of the American home market.
- IBM and IBM-compatible machines have a 59 percent market share (1991).

COMPUTERS

100% American made and owned:

- Cumulus™ Computer

American-owned, and over 50% American parts and/or labor:

- IBM
- Apple
- Tandy
- Dell
- Compaq
- AST Advantage (computer only)
- Datacomp
- Apple Powerbook Notebook Computer (some stock)

American-owned, using less than 50% American parts and/or labor:

- Packard Bell Legend 730
- Packard Bell Legend VIII
- Packard Bell Computer Notebook
- Laser® Pal 386SX
- Cumulus™ 386 Notebook Computer
- Apple Macintosh Classic, Macintosh LC
- Apple Powerbook Notebook Computer

Foreign-owned, using American parts and/or labor:

- Everex
- NEC America Inc.
- Decision Data Computer Corp.
- Modular Computer Systems
- Evans & Southerland Computer Corp.
- Memorex-Telex

Foreign-owned, foreign parts and/or labor:

- Leading Edge 386 sx
- Epson
- Logitec
- Mitsubishi
- Panasonic
- Ricoh
- Samsung
- Sharp
- Sony
- Suntel Computers
- Toshiba
- Wyse Technology
- Xetel Corp.

COMPUTER SOFTWARE

The computer software industry is as close to an all-American industry as any you'll find in the high-tech world. As a patriotic consumer, you'll have no problem easily meeting your software needs with American products. American innovation, creativity, and even playfulness find some of their finest expressions in the programs written for personal computers. How good is American software? Well, it's good enough that more than $4 billion worth is "pirated" (illegally copied and sold) in Europe alone, with even more piracy in the Far East. American software developers are prolific and impressive. As tools for the home office, computers are vital. The right software is even more important because it utilizes the computer's power to meet your needs.

Word Processing Software

When you're shopping for word processing software, think in terms of your own uses—simpler may be better (and less expensive). For PCs, WordPerfect is the most popular word processing software. However, Microsoft Word and several other word processors are also highly rated. Check with computer magazines, which track and review the latest versions of software (a constantly changing scene) for their recommendations. For Macs, Microsoft Word is very popular, but there are several fine alternatives, notably Mac-Write and WriteNow. All are American designed and manufactured.

Integrated Software

An interesting group of software products for your home office is integrated software. These programs include the capabilities to perform several tasks in one package, which means you don't have to buy as many programs. Integrated software typically includes modules for word processing, communications, database management, and spreadsheets. So you can write, keep detailed records of business and finance, communicate with other computers and on-line services (if you have a modem), and more—all at a very attractive price. The main drawback of integrated software is that it offers fewer functions in each module than an individual program such as Microsoft Word. However, for most of us, there's more than enough available on integrated packages. Microsoft Works,

Lotus-Works, and PFS: First Choice are big in the PC-integrated software market. For the Mac crowd, Microsoft Works and Claris Works are excellent. Integrated software is one of the best deals in the high-tech world, generally priced at $200 or less.

Database Management Software

Database management software allows you to deal with tremendous volumes of information. The real question is, do you need to deal with tremendous volumes of information? If not, your needs may be met with integrated software (see above). One of the best uses for database software, simple or complex, is keeping good records of your income and expenses for the nice people at the IRS. For heavy-duty database management, dBase IV, FoxBase, and Paradox are major PC programs; Excel is the leader of the Macs. A specialized group of database programs are designed for Contact Management—to help you keep track of the folks you deal with in business. They're specifically set up for you to easily refer to clients' or associates' names, addresses, and special notes, such as their birthdays or favorite colors. ACT! is such a program, available both in PC and Mac versions. A Mac product, TouchBase, comes well recommended.

Bookkeeping Software

Bookkeeping is a major chore that can be made easier by clever (and inexpensive) software such as the wildly popular Quicken. Created by Intuit, an American company, Quicken is available in both PC and Mac versions. It can keep track of where the money is going, write checks, and even share information with popular tax software to help you when April 15 draws near.

Art and Design Software

Software for drawing, painting, and graphic design is also widely available for your home office. With graphic design software, it is now possible to design handsome brochures, newsletters, business cards, and more on your personal computer. Again, you'll find that buying American is easy, as virtually everything out there is 100 percent American.

American Buying Pattern

- Americans purchase more than $5 billion worth of software each year.
- Sales of word processing software are more than $1 billion in the United States alone.
- Spreadsheet software sales exceed 2.5 million units each year with a sales total of more than $900 million.
- Sales of Windows software are 8 million units and growing.

COMPUTER SOFTWARE

100% American made and owned:

- WordPerfect
- Word
- Microsoft Works
- MacWrite
- Claris Works
- Adobe Systems/Postscript
- Tandy
- Strategic Simulations, Inc.
- Excel
- Parker Brothers
- Swift Professional®
- Lotus
- Quicken
- Write Now
- Lotus Works
- Touch Base
- ACT!

American-owned, and over 50% American parts and/or labor:

- Broderbund®
- Individual Software Incorporated
- Sierra®
- ActiVision®
- MicroProse
- Interplay®
- Intuit

American-owned, using less than 50% American parts and/or labor

Foreign-owned, using American parts and/or labor:

- Grolier Publishing
- Boston Software Publishers
- Virgin Games

Foreign-owned, foreign parts and/or labor:

- Applied Information Software
- Logitech
- RightSoft/Rightwriter
- Program Systems
- Sphere Software
- Tindall Associates
- Tomcat Computer Corp.
- Zortech
- Data Architects Systems
- MBP

COMPUTER PRINTERS

Once you've created something on your personal computer, you'll most likely want to print it out. You can choose from low-cost dot-matrix printers, which provide you with printed copy that's okay but not terrific in appearance, or ink-jet and laser printers, which provide a more professional look to your printed page. Ink-jet printers use a technology developed in part by Hewlett-Packard of Palo Alto, California. These printers literally spray ink onto a page with excellent results. Laser printers use heat to burn letters on to paper. Both the average ink-jet printer and laser printer offer sharp-looking print quality. Dot-matrix printers (virtually all foreign-made) are fading from the scene.

Hewlett-Packard is an American company that has combined quality and innovation with an enlightened regard for its almost 90,000 employees in the United States and overseas. Started in 1939 by Stanford-trained engineers Dave Packard and Bill Hewlett on a shoestring bank account of $538, H-P chalked up worldwide income of $14.7 billion in 1991. A constant theme at H-P has been electronic innovation. Our astronauts relied on H-P diodes, switches, and precision instruments when they landed on the moon in 1969. When it was introduced in 1972, the H-P-35 handheld scientific calculator made the engineer's slide rule a thing of the past.

For home-office use, you might find the Hewlett-Packard Desk-Jet/DeskWriter family of printers very attractive. These ink-jet printers have achieved worldwide popularity in just a few years because they combine excellent print quality and affordability. Typically, you can find a DeskJet or DeskWriter for under $500; Hewlett-Packard has worked hard to keep its pricing attractive. DeskJet printers serve IBM and IBM-compatible computers; DeskWriter printers serve the Apple Macintosh computer line. For a bit more, color versions of both printers are available. The DeskJet printer currently is the most popular printer in the world. Best of all, the DeskJet/DeskWriter printers sold here are born and bred in the United States. Manufacturing takes place in Vancouver, Washington; more than 90 percent of the components are American-made.

American Buying Pattern

- Americans spent close to $12 billion on printers in 1991.
- Sales of laser printers were responsible for 84 percent of the non-impact printer market, which grew to nearly $8 billion in 1991.
- Experts estimate a 7 percent increase in the total American printer market in 1992, with sales of more than $13 billion.

COMPUTER PRINTERS

100% American made and owned:

- Hewlett-Packard DeskWriter, DeskJet
- IBM PS/1

American-owned, and over 50% American parts and/or labor:

- Hewlett-Packard LaserJet II, LaserJet III
- Lexmark LaserPrinter
- IBM LP-5E

American-owned, using less than 50% American parts and/or labor:

- Apple StyleWriter
- Hewlett-Packard Laser II P Plus
- Sears SR #000 Dot Matrix Printer
- Sears SR 5000 Dot Matrix Printer

Foreign-owned, using American parts and/or labor:

- Fujitsu America Inc.
- Memory Systems Div (MSD)
- Epson Portland Inc.
- Hitachi Computer Products Inc.

Foreign-owned, foreign parts and/or labor:

- Panasonic KX-1123, KX-P2180, KX-P4410
- Citizen GSX 140
- Okidata 800 Laser Printer
- Epson Action Printer 2000
- Epson Action Printer 3250
- Epson Action Printer 5000
- Seikosha SP 2000 Plus

MODEMS AND FAX MODEMS

Communication—between two or more computers, between computers and on-line database services offering a wealth of information, and between computers and fax machines—is now possible with modems and fax modems, devices installed in or attached to your computer. And there are American choices for these products—among them, companies such as Hayes, Intel, and Global Village Communications. Your home office can easily be plugged in to the world outside through the phone system, providing you with sophisticated communications capabilities that up until recently were available to only a wealthy few.

Modems transmit and receive data between computers via telephone lines. This means your PC can transmit information to any other computer by turning information into a common denominator. It can also receive information the same way. This means you can communicate with any computer in the world from your home office, provided the other computer also has a modem. The speed at which data is transmitted is expressed as bps (bits per second). Virtually all modems now transmit at a minimum of 2400 bps. Higher numbers mean faster transmission and lower phone bills, provided the computer on the other end can receive as fast as you can send. If it's slower than your modem, your modem will send at a speed both computers share. Some modems come with communications software included. Other modems come without such software, meaning added expense. Shop for value and heed the advice of friends, computer user groups, and major computer publications.

Modems can be used for much more than sending your computer-generated documents. Leave it to American ingenuity to come up with on-line services such as America Online, AT&T Mail, CompuServe, GEnie, MCI Mail, Prodigy, The Well, and Windows Online. These communications networks can accommodate you in everything from offering a forum to discuss world affairs to booking your next flight to Chicago. On-line services can literally provide news, weather, sports, financial reports, encyclopedic information, games, and even the opportunity to meet other people through your computer. But they're not free. Typically, there's a small monthly fee plus hourly charges for your use of the service.

Fax modems provide the modem capabilities discussed above

with the desirable addition of fax technology. This enables your computer to act as a sending or receiving fax. There are advantages, especially in sending faxes. Computer-generated faxes are crisper-looking than those sent by fax machines because they don't have to be "scanned" by a fax machine before sending. And they offer some features not available in low-cost fax machines. For instance, you can create a directory of people you send to regularly. When you want to send a fax, just select their names from a menu and send directly—the computer does the dialing. You can set your computer to send faxes late at night, when phone rates are lower. And you can print out the faxes you receive in the computer at your printer's best resolution. You may find that a fax modem is great for sending documents created by the computer and a separate fax machine serves better for receiving and sending documents not created in your computer. The fax is now one of the facts of life. Consider a fax modem or fax machine for your home office.

Modems are available from a wide range of American-owned companies. Two important players are Hayes, a leader in modem technology, and Intel, a major supplier of the chips that power PCs. However, a number of other American companies are in the modem business. Again, check with friends, user groups and computer publications for recommendations. Many modems include both American and foreign components, as do computers. Look at the product to see if it's made in the United States before you buy.

Fax modems are also available from Intel—their product is called SatisFAXtion. It's only available for PCs. A well-regarded Mac fax modem is called TelePort FullFax and is made by Global Village Communications in Menlo Park, California.

FAX MACHINES

In just a few years, fax machines have gone from a high-end corporate gizmo to an affordable part of small businesses and home offices. Some fast-food restaurants even take orders over the fax! For your home office, the fax machine provides immediate communication, bypassing the mail service (which can take days) and overnight delivery services (expensive). You and your contacts can work with documents quickly and effectively using fax technology. All you need for a fax is a phone line. Many fax machines can share phone lines with a regular phone or do double duty with the phone attatched to the fax. A fax is one item likely to pay for itself in a hurry.

While the good news is that fax machines are offering more for less every day, the bad news is that, for patriotic consumers, there aren't many American-made fax machines. Ironically, fax technology is an American invention, originally developed by AT&T in the 1920s. Now, even AT&T fax machines are made in Japan. On the bright side, the "brain" of more than half the fax machines in use was made by an American company, Rockwell International. Rockwell supplies the computer modem circuits that allow the fax machine to send and receive digital information across phone lines.

You will see fax machines with American-sounding names like Canon, Sharp, and even the names of some local phone companies. Don't be fooled—virtually all fax machines are foreign-made. One American-made line of fax machines is available from Hewlett-Packard. Their products offer you very high quality but are not low-priced. H-P fax machines use ink-jet printing on plain paper (instead of the usual slick, thermal fax paper) to provide a high-quality document. An H-P fax machine is your best American-made alternative to the imports.

American Buying Pattern

- Modems have soared in popularity as prices have dropped and speed has dramatically increased in recent years.
- The retail dollar value of facsimile equipment in 1990 was approximately $1.6 billion.
- On average, a fax machine will last 8 years.
- Experts predict that more than 100,000 fax machines will need to be replaced in 1992.
- In 1990, roughly 6 percent of American households owned a fax machine.

MODEMS, FAX MODEMS, AND FAX MACHINES

100% American made and owned

American-owned, and over 50% American parts and/or labor:

- Rockwell International
- Hewlett-Packard Plain Paper Fax
- Intel
- Hayes
- Global Village Communications

American-owned, using less than 50% American parts and/or labor:

- Pitney Bowes
- AT&T
- Lanier Worldwide
- Monroe
- Swintec
- Tandy
- Xerox

Foreign-owned, using American parts and/or labor:

- Canon Fax-2705
- Canon Fax-A501

Foreign-owned, foreign parts and/or labor:

- Sharp FO 130
- Panasonic KX50, KX-155, KX-215
- Murata M 1100 Fax, Phone, and Copier
- Murata 1500
- Murata 1900
- Brother IntelliFax 600, 700
- Sharp
- Ricoh
- Toshiba
- AEG Olympia
- Epson
- Gestetner
- Konica
- Samsung
- Sony

TELEPHONES AND ANSWERING MACHINES

The telephone and answering machine are an integral part of any home office. Gone are the days when you had to rent a phone from the phone company, which was the only game in town. Today there are a tremendous variety of phones and answering machines available. They can be cheap or expensive, basic or full of exotic features. The trick is buying American. Much of the telephone equipment sold in the United States is foreign-made or made with a high percentage of foreign components. Even some American companies are really just selling foreign goods with their name on it.

Two United States manufacturers, Comdial and ITT/Cortelco, still make phones in America. For the record, ITT/Cortelco is owned by Alacatel, a French corporation. For those who want to take the phone on the road, look for the name Motorola in your cellular phone search. More than 50 years old, Motorola sells about 25 percent of the world's cellular phones.

American Buying Pattern

- In 1990, more than 40 percent of all American households owned an answering machine.
- American manufacturers shipped more than $31 million in telephone answering machines in 1990.
- Out of 94 million American households, over 93 percent had a telephone in 1990.
- In 1990, Americans made over 1.5 billion local calls, and 162 million long-distance calls each day.

TELEPHONES AND ANSWERING MACHINES

100% American made and owned

American-owned, and over 50% American parts and/or labor:

- Comdial Corp.
- AT&T Partner Phone
- AT&T Merlin® Phone System
- AT&T Transportable Cellular
- Motorola Cellular Phone
- Motorola Cordless Phone

American-owned, using less than 50% American parts and/or labor:

- AT&T Two Line Speakerphone
- GE Two Line Speakerphone
- Southwestern Bell Freedom Phone
- BellSouth 236V
- AT&T 1337
- AT&T 1504 Remote Answering System Phone
- AT&T Trimline® 210
- AT&T Traditional 100
- AT&T Memory 710
- AT&T Digital Answering System
- GE Memory Phone
- GE Answer Phone
- GE Cordless
- Sears Trimstyle Phone
- BellSouth Cordless 667 and 675

Foreign-owned, using American parts and/or labor:

- Cortelco Trendline Phone
- Cortelco Citation Phone
- Cortelco Tribute Phone

(continued)

- Citizen Systems
- Fujitsui GTE Business Systems
- Mitsubishi Consumer Electronics
- Northern Telecom Electronic Inc.
- Oki Telecom Inc.
- Uniden Corp of America

Foreign-owned, foreign parts and/or labor:

- Panasonic KX-73145
- Code-A-Phone Model 1650
- PhoneMate 7400
- PhoneMate 3950
- PhoneMate 8250
- Panasonic KX-T 3710 Cordless
- Sony SPP 75 Cordless
- Panasonic EASA-Phone

TYPEWRITERS AND WORD PROCESSORS

If you ever took typing in school, you probably learned on a classic American typewriter such as the IBM Selectric. Every office had them. Now, typewriters are losing ground to inexpensive personal computers, but they still have their place. Typewriters are great for quick notes, envelopes, school reports, and other modest chores. These days, most typewriters are electronic. Full-featured typewriters often have "memory" and even spelling checkers. Generally, they're solid, reliable pieces of equipment.

As this book went to press, Smith-Corona, the last American manufacturer (48% British-owned) of popularly priced typewriters, announced it was moving its manufacturing facilities to Mexico. IBM is about to become the only United States manufacturer of typewriters for your home office. Though its Personal Wheelwriter and Wheelwriter 10 Series II aren't bargain-basement priced, IBM has a long tradition of building first class typewriters. So, if you're looking to buy an inexpensive typewriter for a home office, the choices now are all foreign-made. Sad, since typewriters were yet another American invention.

American Buying Pattern

- In 1990, Americans spent $1,237,579,200 on typewriters.
- American manufacturers exported over 270,000 standard typewriters, valued at more than $62 million, in 1990.

TYPEWRITERS AND WORD PROCESSORS

100% American made and owned:

- Smith-Corona PWP 770
  (This will change soon with production moving to Mexico.)
- IBM Personal Wheelwriter
- IBM Wheelwriter 10 Series II
- Smith-Corona PWP 4200
- Smith-Corona PWP 1200
- Sears LXI Word Processing Typewriter

American-owned, and over 50% American parts and/or labor:

- IBM
- Monroe
- Swintec
- Tandy
- Wang Labs
- Xerox

American-owned, using less than 50% American parts and/or labor:

- Sears SR 1000 C Electronic Typewriter
- Smith-Corona DX 4500 Word Processing Typewriter
- Smith-Corona XL 1800

Foreign-owned, using American parts and/or labor:

- Brother GX 8000, GX 8500, GX 9000
- Brother WP-3400
- Brother WP-1500
- Brother AX-250 Electronic Typewriter
- Brother GX 6000, GX 7000 Electronic Typewriter

Foreign-owned, foreign parts and/or labor:

- Canon Star Writer 60, Star Writer 80
- Canon ES 3, ES 23
- Sharp PA3020 II
- Brother Power-Note Laptop Word Processor
- Panasonic W 905
- Panasonic Laptop Word Processor
- Kenwood
- Olympia/Olympic
- Sharp
- TA Adler Royal
- AB Dick
- NEC
- Royal

OFFICE FURNITURE

You have to put everything somewhere in your home office, including yourself! Where do you sit to do your work? In the past, an old desk and a hard chair were the norm. These days, the word "ergonomics" is in fashion—in plain talk it means healthy comfort. After investing in computers, phones, and other high-tech gadgets, let's not forget to invest in ourselves. Sore backs, stiff necks, and possible long-term physical problems are a high price to pay for the wrong home office furniture. Studies show that discomfort is distracting, too, so good office furniture is also an investment in your productivity.

Finding sturdy, comfortable American-made furniture is easy for the patriotic consumer. American furniture makers pioneered standards of quality and production that the world has copied. Today, they enjoy most of the American market, and with good reason. American furniture makers deliver the goods!

For your home office, your primary needs are likely to be a desk, chair(s), bookcase, computer and printer desk, and filing cabinet. Let's take a look at two American companies devoted to meeting those needs.

In the midst of Ohio corn fields, you'll find Sauder Woodworking Co. in Archbold, Ohio. Founded by Erie Sauder in 1934, Sauder Woodworking is still a family-owned enterprise, employing 1,900 local people. Erie's son, Maynard, is its current president. His son, Kevin, is director of marketing. Clearly, they're doing a lot of things right at Sauder, as 1992 sales will exceed $340 million. In fact, they get fan mail from customers. One 83-year-old man said, "I am pleased that we [Americans] can outperform [foreign competition]." One couple wrote Sauder to say "your workmanship is something to be proud of and is an example for U.S.A. manufacturers to follow." And yet another happy customer said he "just had to write you to congratulate you on renewing my faith in American products."

For the home office, Sauder offers a wide range of attractive, affordable furniture that comes in ready-to-assemble (RTA) form. Sauder is the world's largest manufacturer of RTA furniture. All Sauder furniture is American-made and more than 90 percent of components are American, too. Don't worry about putting Sauder's furniture together. Sauder's reputation is based on things fitting snugly with easy-to-follow instructions. To quote one customer, "I have never seen a better kit, nor a better set of directions."

Sauder offers desks, computer desks and work centers, computer carts, printer carts, printer/typewriter stands, file cabinets and file carts, bookshelves, desktop organizers, and storage cabinets. Most are wood-tone, using wood veneers and other wood products. They look great and they do the job. Sauder is a good choice for the patriotic consumer.

Muscatine, Iowa, is the home of HON Industries, whose line of American-made office furniture runs the gamut from posh to budget-minded. Founded in 1944, HON's original name, Home-O-Nize, was created for a company aimed at revolutionizing kitchen cabinetry. A few years down the road, the company found its niche and stayed there. Today HON sales top $600 million a year. The company employs 5,600 Americans in 11 different states. More than 95 percent of HON Industries' products are made in the United States and virtually all components are American-made.

HON products have been enjoyed by some well-known consumers, including nine United States presidents, who chose the company's premier Gunlocke furniture for the Oval Office. Gunlocke products include fine desks, tables, and ergonomically designed chairs, all made with hand-selected lumber and high-grade wood veneers. HON's Corry-Hiebert Company makes high-quality metal desks, seating, and filing cabinets. Holga, Inc., another HON company, makes office storage products. The HON Company, the branch of HON Industries providing the widest range of office furniture, began with a simple metal recipe box from parent Home-O-Nize.

Today, HON offers attractive, reasonably priced desks, chairs, computer furniture, and filing systems. The XLM Company, a HON subsidiary, creates Office Partner brand products specifically for the home office and small business markets. Office Partner products include files and desk-top systems, which integrate file and desk in a single unit, a good idea if space is tight in your home office. Finally, another HON company, Ring King Visibles, Inc., provides diskette storage trays, work station accessories, sound enclosures, printer stands, and even rubber bands.

Other highly rated American manufacturers of home office furniture are O'Sullivan and Bush.

American Buying Pattern

- Each year we spend more than $1.3 billion on home office furniture.
- American-made home office furniture accounts for 90 percent of the home office market.
- Americans bought more than $5.5 billion in metal office furniture in 1990.

OFFICE FURNITURE

100% American made and owned:

- Sauder furniture
- HON furniture
- O'Sullivan file cabinets, credenzas
- Maxi Rack shelves

American-owned, and over 50% American parts and/or labor:

- Sauder furniture

American-owned, using less than 50% American parts and/or labor

Foreign-owned, using American parts and/or labor:

- Gusdorf bookcases
- Stendig Inc.
- The Butler Group
- Kruegger Inc.
- Junoflex Systems
- Girsberger Industries
- Hanson Office Products (Furniture)

Foreign-owned, foreign parts and/or labor:

- Bestar furniture
- CTS Products file cabinets
- Smart Business Home Office Work Center

OFFICE ACCESSORIES

Adhesive tape, paper clips, and even file folders are the little things that hold our home offices together. American companies know what we need because America wrote the book on organizing offices.

Let's start with a sticky subject. The 3-M Company in St. Paul, Minnesota, brings you Scotch tape, masking tape, strapping tape, and packing tape among the 66,000 products they sell for yearly revenues of more than $13 billion. And let's not forget everyone's favorite sticky invention, Post-it Notes. 3-M chemical engineer Arthur Fry turned a glue failure into a runaway success after spending nine months at the task. Fry was looking for a marker for his church hymnal that would adhere without damaging the page. He remembered a co-worker's unsuccessful attempt to create a new adhesive—the stuff just wasn't that sticky. Today, sales of Post-it Notes, available in many shapes, colors, and sizes, top $45 million; Fry has even been lauded in *People* magazine. Fry didn't rest on his laurels. He has since developed shelf-arranger tape for libraries and gift-wrap bows.

It's not easy to find American-made pens, especially the disposable variety. When you shop for pens, be sure and look for ones made by American companies like Papermate, A.T. Cross, Mark Cross, and Waterman. They need all the help they can get to compete with foreign giants like Bic, Parker, Pentel, and Pilot.

Then there are paper clips. United States steel and American know-how combine in these vital office products. American companies such as ACCO International of Wheeling, Illinois, turn out a spectrum of sizes and colors of paper clips by the millions.

Globe-Weiss of St. Louis, Missouri, makes many of the manila file folders we use to keep track of everything from the car's service record to our latest project. And we have to label those files. That's where Avery products come in. This American company has labels for your files, computer printers, and a lot more. Liquid Paper Co. of Boston helps us clean up mistakes in a hurry. There are plenty of fine American paper suppliers such as Stuart Hall of Kansas City, Missouri. To staple them together, take a look at the quality of American-made Swingline staplers and staples. Don't forget to look for "Made In America" when you're buying pens, pencils, typewriter/computer ribbons and cartridges, and batteries.

THE GARAGE

Standing alone or attached to the house, two-car or no car at all (if it's jammed with our "treasures"), the all-American garage is an empty space we can fill as we like. The garage is also where many of us go to tinker and where many American dreams begin, for it's the humble birthplace of such legendary American companies as Apple Computer, Hewlett-Packard, and Harley-Davidson.

Since the garage has lots of uses and plenty of room to fill, let's be sure we're not filling it with imported goods. With its rich entrepreneurial legacy and big-ticket items, the garage is a logical spot to use our buying power to begin buying back the American dream.

Take an Inventory

Look inside the average American garage and you'll be amazed at the variety of its contents. There's likely to be a car or motorcycle, a bicycle or two, some golf clubs, a box of tools, a few lawn chairs, a barbecue, maybe a lawn mower and some other gardening equipment, and much more, depending on the owner's hobbies and interests. Americans have a lot of money invested in their garages, but how much of what we spend goes into American-made products?

Now's a good time to look around your shelves and workbench. A close inspection of your power drill may tell you it was made in China. Your bicycles may have come from Japan. But if the tennis balls you love to lob on the weekends are made by Penn, they're as American as they come. From cars to tools, we'll show you that there are plenty of ways to be a patriotic consumer when it comes to filling your garage.

Don't Be Fooled

Are you in the market for a new American car? How about a

brand-new Ford Crown Victoria or a Mercury Grand Marquis? Sorry, both are imported from Canada. Refusing to even look at Japanese imports like Nissan Sentra? Surprise! It was probably made at a plant in Tennessee. And that Geo Prizm at your General Motors dealer is actually a hybrid made in California by GM in a joint venture with Toyota.

The fact is, it's almost impossible to buy a 100 percent made-in-America car these days. At least 25 percent of the components in any domestic model are purchased outside the country. And profits on the highly rated Jaguar may actually be ending up in the hands of American owners like Ford.

Maybe you're shopping for a bicycle made in America. Don't let an American brand name fool you. Eager to take advantage of lower labor costs abroad, some major companies prefer to produce their models in countries like Taiwan, South Korea, and China. Schwinn now sources most of its bikes in Asia. Some firms that assemble bikes here buy their frames in other countries. Always check the label before making your choice.

Comparison Shopping

You don't have to be an avid reader of *Car & Driver Magazine* to realize that the quality of American-made vehicles has increased dramatically over the past few years. Just look at the number of Chrysler minivans on the road, listen to the way their owners rave about them, and you can see that the times have changed for the better regarding the quality of American cars.

You'll find that American cars are often less expensive than imports—even when they are accessorized with air conditioning, cruise control, or a CD player. You'll also be delighted to learn that parts for domestic cars often run half the price of those used for imports.

When it comes to home improvement projects, you'll be right at "home" with an impressive selection of high-quality hand and power tools made right here in America. Companies like Black & Decker, Porter-Cable, and Milwaukee produce the best quality drills, sanders, and saws in the world. Sears guarantees its American-made line of Craftsman hand tools for life.

The Payoff

When one in seven Americans is employed in some way by the

automobile industry, it's easy to see what the payoff is for buying American-made cars. The garage is one place where, by buying American-made products, we can make a big difference in our economy in a short time and, in the long run, improve the lives of all Americans.

• Industry experts estimate that Americans will replace 5.4 million lawnmowers in 1992. If everyone purchased a $500 American-made machine, instead of an import model, 67,500 new jobs could be created.

CARS

No other treasure in our garage is more written about, discussed, or argued over than the automobile. Until the early 1950s, the basic American choices were simple: Ford, Chrysler, and General Motors. The Big Three. American cars, American parts, assembled by American workers.

The confusion began in the 1950s when the Volkswagen Bug nosed its way into garages coast to coast. Ever since then, major importers have continued to carve out a bigger share of our nation's $200-billion-a-year auto market. Today, the Japanese alone control roughly a third of this market.

Japanese and European cars have earned a reputation for reliability, fuel efficiency, and low operating cost. This competition has hurt our automakers. But it has also prompted them to come up with better cars, well worth your consideration. Not only are American models often the best value on the market, many are at the top of their respective class.

Until Congress passes proposed legislation requiring all American cars to be labeled with details on the country of origin, you may have trouble figuring where a possible purchase was built. Further complicating this problem is the fact that some manufacturers split their model runs between domestic and overseas plants.

To make your shopping easier, we've identified a number of highly regarded models built in our country. Buying one of these cars supports our autoworkers and helps revive this crucial domestic industry. All are excellent values.

If you haven't owned an American brand for a while, or are getting into the market for the first time, why not rent one for a weekend? Even better, talk with friends and neighbors who own models you're considering.

When shopping, don't just listen to dealers. Do some reading. Check the annual spring automotive issue of *Consumer Reports* or pick up the *Consumer Buying Guide*. By comparing the Japanese, European, and American makes you'll see just how much the quality of our cars has increased in recent years.

Among the models we urge you to consider are the compacts Plymouth Acclaim and Dodge Colt. Both lines include 4-door sedans with driver-side air bags and plenty of passenger and cargo space. Rebates and option-package discounts make it possible to buy a model with automatic transmission, air conditioning, and antilock brakes for less than $15,000. Also worthy of your consideration is the General Motors Saturn.

The mid-size Ford Taurus and Mercury Sable are also highly rated. Aerodynamic styling, roomy passenger compartments, driver-side air bags (a passenger-side air bag is optional), and front-wheel drive help explain their popularity. The full-size Buick LeSabre and Oldsmobile Eighty-Eight also offer front-wheel drive. Like the luxury Cadillac line, these cars compare favorably with higher-priced imports.

If you have a large family, be sure to consider the Dodge Caravan and the Plymouth Voyager. Equipped with a driver-side air bag, they come with such options as antilock brakes and integrated child seats. These roomy vehicles also have one of the best warranties in the industry.

Finally, if you do a lot of back-road driving, consider the Ford Explorer. This smooth-riding 4-wheel-drive vehicle comes with plenty of cargo capacity, as well as antilock rear brakes.

There you have it, an impressive selection in all price ranges that is likely to woo even the most skeptical consumer back to the American car lot. Welcome home!

American Buying Pattern

- In 1990, the Ford Taurus was the second biggest seller in the United States (more than 300,000 cars). The Honda Accord was the number one seller (more than 400,000 cars sold).
- In 1990, the United States produced a total of 9,780,236 passenger cars, trucks, and buses.
- Air conditioning is an option chosen by 85 percent of Americans who buy an American car.
- In 1990, the average American auto still on the road was 7.8 years old.
- Thirty percent of American cars on the road are 10 years old or more.
- Thirty-four percent of all households in the United States have one vehicle in the driveway. More than 36 percent of American households have two vehicles.

CARS

100% American made and owned:

American-owned, and over 50% American parts and/or labor:

- Buick LeSabre
- Buick Park Avenue
- Buick Riviera
- Buick Roadmaster
- Buick Skylark
- Cadillac Brougham
- Cadillac DeVille
- Cadillac Eldorado
- Cadillac Fleetwood
- Cadillac Seville
- Chevrolet Beretta
- Chevrolet Camaro
- Chevrolet Caprice
- Chevrolet Cavalier
- Chevrolet Corsica
- Chevrolet Corvette
- Chrysler Imperial
- Chrysler LeBaron coupe
- Chrysler New Yorker
- Dodge Shadow
- Dodge Daytona
- Dodge Dynasty
- Dodge Spirit
- Dodge Viper
- Ford Escort
- Ford Mustang
- Ford Probe
- Ford Taurus
- Ford Tempo
- Ford Thunderbird
- Geo Prizm
- Lincoln (all models)
- Mercury Cougar
- Mercury Sable
- Mercury Topaz
- Oldsmobile (all models)
- Plymouth Acclaim
- Plymouth Sundance
- Pontiac Bonneville
- Pontiac Firebird
- Pontiac Grand Am
- Pontiac Grand Prix
- Pontiac Sunbird
- Saturn (all models)

American-owned, using less than 50% American parts and/or labor:

- Buick Regal
- Cadillac Allante
- Chevrolet Lumina
- Chrysler Concorde
- Dodge Colt
- Dodge Intrepid
- Dodge Monaco
- Dodge Stealth
- Eagle Premier
- Eagle Talon
- Eagle Vision
- Ford Festiva

(continued)

- Ford Tempo
- Jaguar (Ford)
- Lamborghini (Chrysler)
- Mercury Capri
- Mercury Topaz
- Mercury Tracer
- Plymouth Colt
- Plymouth Colt Vista
- Plymouth Laser
- Pontiac LeMans

Foreign-owned, using American parts and/or labor:

- Honda Civic
- Honda Accord coupe, wagon
- Hyundai Sonata
- Mazda 626 (1992)
- Mazda MX-6 (1992)
- Mitsubishi Eclipse
- Mitsubishi Mirage 4-door
- Nissan Sentra
- Subaru Legacy
- Toyota Camry
- Toyota Corolla sedan
- Volkswagen Golf, Jetta
- Volvo 740 wagon
- Volvo 940 wagon

Foreign-owned, foreign parts and/or labor:

- Acura
- Alfa Romeo
- Aston Martin
- Audi
- Bentley
- BMW
- Daihatsu
- Ferrari
- Honda Accord 4-door
- Honda Civic 4-door
- Honda CRX
- Honda Prelude
- Hyundai Elantra
- Hyundai Excel
- Hyundai S-coupe
- Hyundai Sonata
- Infiniti
- Lexus
- Lotus
- Maserati
- Mazda MX-3
- Mazda MX-5 Miata
- Mazda Protege
- Mazda 929
- Mazda RX-7
- Mazda 323
- Mercedes-Benz
- Mitsubishi Diamante
- Mitsubishi Expo
- Mitsubishi Galant
- Mitsubishi Mirage 3-door
- Mitsubishi Precis
- Mitsubishi 3000GT
- Nissan NX 1600/2000
- Nissan Maxima
- Nissan Sentra
- Nissan Stanza
- Nissan 300ZX
- Nissan 240SX
- Porsche *(continued)*

- Rolls-Royce
- Saab 900
- Saab 9000
- Subaru Justy
- Subaru Legacy
- Subaru Loyale
- Subaru SVX
- Suzuki Swift
- Toyota Camry
- Toyota Celica
- Toyota Corolla sedan
- Toyota Corolla wagon
- Toyota Cressida
- Toyota MR2
- Toyota Paseo

- Toyota Supra
- Toyota Tercel
- Volkswagen Cabriolet
- Volkswagen Corrado
- Volkswagen Fox
- Volkswagen Jetta
- Volkswagen Passat
- Volvo 240
- Volvo 740 wagon
- Volvo 740 sedan
- Volvo 940 wagon
- Volvo 940 sedan
- Volvo 960
- Yugo

MOTORCYCLES

No other object in our garage gives us such a distinctly American alternative as the motorcycle. Harley-Davidson is the only manufacturer of a popularly priced motorcycle whose product stands out as purely American-designed and American-made.

In 1901, William S. Harley, age 21, teamed up with his boyhood friend Arthur Davidson, 20, to turn their "tinkering" into practical use. The two young men worked at the same manufacturing company, where Harley was a draftsman and Davidson a pattern maker. Another draftsman, a German who worked with the two young men, knew about European motorcycles and the gasoline engine. Combined, they used their talents to craft an American dream into a superb American product and a legendary American success story. Part of the legend says that the first Harley-Davidson carburetor was made from a tomato can, and that the first spark plug was the size of a doorknob.

Just how popular are Harley-Davidsons? A distributor in the Northeast recently told a prospective customer that he could not order a 1992 motorcycle; they were all sold out.

Motorcycle riding is both a popular recreational activity and source of transportation. Close to 31 million Americans operated a motorcycle, scooter, or ATV (all-terrain vehicle) in 1990. Motorcycles, scooters, and ATVs are also used in such diverse activities as agriculture, law enforcement, and land resources management.

American Buying Pattern

- There are more than 9,600 retail outlets selling new motorcycles or motorcycle-related services, parts, and accessories.
- Motorcycle retail outlets, in 1990, employed some 46,000 people at an estimated payroll of $756 million.
- In 1990, estimated retail sales of new motorcycles, scooters, and ATVs were 462,000 units, valued at $1.8 billion.
- Harley-Davidson, with a 17.4 percent market share, ranks third in the United States motorcycle market.
- An estimated 140,000 motorcycles and ATVs were made in America in 1990. Imports totalled 169,000.

MOTORCYCLES

100% American made and owned

American-owned, and over 50% American parts and/or labor:

- Harley-Davidson Sportster®
- Harley-Davidson Dyna Glide™
- Harley-Davidson Softail®
- Harley-Davidson Touring Series
- Buell WestWind RS1200

Please note Harley-Davidson motorcycles are estimated at 90 percent American-made. Buell estimates its motorcycles are 95 percent American-made.

American-owned, using less than 50% American parts and/or labor

Foreign-owned, using American parts and/or labor:

- Honda GoldWing
- Honda Shadow 1100
- Honda Four Tracks 300, 200, and 90
- Kawasaki ATV
- Kawasaki Police Special
- Kawasaki ZX 600C, ZX600D, ZG1000A, and ZG1200B

Foreign-owned, foreign parts and/or labor:

- BMW
- Honda
- Husaberg
- Husky/Husqvarna

- Kawasaki
- KTM
- Suzuki
- Yamaha

BICYCLES

Bicycles used to be a child's toy or a simple and inexpensive way to get from here to there. Not so today. Now they're an Olympic sport, a fabulous way to keep healthy, and great way to explore the countryside. If you purchase a bicycle made in America, you'll become a part of one of our nation's great manufacturing success stories. At the same time that demand for high-quality American bikes is soaring abroad, foreign manufacturers are losing market share here. For example, in 1990 exports of American bikes were 146 percent above 1989. Equally encouraging is the fact that foreign bike companies captured only 40 percent of the United States market in 1991, compared with 59 percent in 1987.

With 7.2 million American-made bikes sold in our country each year, it's obvious where our loyalty rests. You can accelerate this trend by insisting on an American make. A number of American cycling firms manufacture everything in the United States.

The best place to begin your research is a neighborhood bike store. Not only are they likely to carry first-rate domestic models, they'll also probably have helpful consumer buying guides and books. You can also get additional suggestions on American-made products from the Bicycle Manufacturers Association in Washington (1–202–944–9297).

You'll be delighted by the climbing power of the new American mountain bikes, which are prized in foreign markets for their durability and comfort. Other alternatives are city bikes built for urban riding and lightweight road bikes made for competition.

Most bicycles priced under $500 have frames made in one of eight plants in Taiwan. Almost all the components—the crank, chain, freewheel, shift levers, and brakes—are made in Japan. While price considerations may tempt you to buy a foreign bike, keep in mind that many of the best riding models are built here. Possibilities include Murray, Huffy, and Roadmaster.

Our country's second-largest maker of cycling products, Murray, is now owned by the British company Tomkins P.L.C. Producing about 3 million bikes last year, their line runs from beginner's bikes, perfect for the training-wheel crowd, to durable mountain bikes. Known for its advance manufacturing techniques, this firm is considered an industry leader. Murray's 65-acre factory has 3,000 employees and the company is currently expanding its capacity.

The mountain, or all-terrain, bike is another important American contribution to the transportation industry. Among the domestic mountain bikes you may want to consider are the products of the Specialized Bike Company, Trek Manufacturing, and Cannondale. Specialized is known for its Rock Hopper and Stumpjumper models.

According to Cannondale's president and founder, Joseph S. Montgomery, "Cannondale began with four dedicated people hand-building bicycle trailers in a crowded loft above a pickle factory." Today, Cannondale is famous for its lightweight aluminum frames, as well as its advanced suspension system. These higher-priced bikes are widely exported to countries in Asia and Europe.

Trek is a high-end firm that makes its 900 line in our country. For over fifteen years, Trek has been designing and crafting high-quality bicycles—from mountain bikes and hybrids to road bikes and tandems. When you see a Trek and the words "Made in the U.S.A." on the frame, you know you're getting quality.

If you're in the market for a truly unique bike and money is no obstacle, you might consider the original Hopalong Cassidy bike. Hopalong Cassidy was a cowboy with his own television series during the mid- to late-1950s. Hoppy's bike was introduced as the "original cowboy bicycle." Made by the D.P. Harris Hardware Manufacturing Company of New York, only 12 are currently available. The Hopalong Cassidy model includes the unique Hopalong medallion and Hopalong signature on the oversized "gas tank," a white diamond and circle chain guard, curved headlights, and push-button horn set into the gas tank. All this can be yours for only $6,000! The price, by the way, includes two D-cell batteries for the horn. Oh, one other thing: professional assembly is recommended.

After you've completed your purchase, make a point of specifying American-made accessories. For example, Bell makes one of the top helmet lines. If you're considering a security lock, you'll have a hard time beating the popular Kryptonite models. And when it comes to biking apparel, you'll find our manufacturers create functional, reasonably priced design.

Your purchase not only helps American industry, it strengthens our bike companies at a time when they are fighting hard for export markets.

American Buying Pattern

- A million more bicycles were sold in 1991 than in 1990.
- The bicycle market—including bikes and related parts and accessories—is worth about $4 billion in annual sales.
- Mountain bike sales rose 250 percent between 1987 and 1990.
- Americans bought a total of 4.6 million bicycles in 1991.
- Most bicycles are purchased at bike shops, followed by department stores and, to a lesser degree, sporting goods stores.

BICYCLES

100% American made and owned:

- Roadmaster 26-inch Stillwater Pass
- Roadmaster 26-inch Skyline Crest
- Cannondale (all models)
- Trek® Single-Track
- Trek® 1100
- Trek® 1200
- Diamond Back Traverse®

American-owned, and over 50% American parts and/or labor:

- Huffy 26-inch Crosswind
- Huffy 26-inch ATB
- Huffy 26-inch Stone Mountain
- Huffy 26-inch Stalker
- Stowe Cycles
- Klein Bicycle
- Spectrum
- Trek® USA (some models)
- Ritchey USA
- Burley Tandem
- Ibis Cycles

American-owned, using less than 50% American parts and/or labor:

- Trek® Multi-Track
- Trek® Antelope
- Roadmaster ATB (some models)
- Rallye® 26-inch Regal, Clearwater, Meridien
- Schwinn (all models except custom ATB)
- Mudy Fox
- Marin Mountain Bikes
- Ross Bicycles USA
- Scott
- GT
- Mongoose Bicycles

- Diamond Back Ambition®, Outlook®
- Diamond Back Apex®, Ultra/Storm®
- Specialized Cross Roads Cruz®

Foreign-owned, using American parts and/or labor:

- Murray ATB
- Murray "Monterey" Cruiser
- Haro Bicycles (adult)
- Raleigh Technium® Bikes

Foreign-owned, foreign parts and/or labor:

- Haro (children's bikes)
- Raleigh (children's bikes)
- Panasonic
- Fuji America
- Cycles Peugeot USA
- Miyata
- Bianchi USA
- Excel Sports
- KHS International
- Rocky Mountain
- Bridgestone Cycles
- Cinelli
- Centurion
- Giant
- Pinarello
- Novara

SPORTING GOODS

Walk into your local sporting-goods store and you'll see what Americans are doing in their spare time. There's everything from baseballs, bats, and gloves to tennis rackets, skis, golf clubs, sleds, footballs, and basketballs. And, of course, it all ends up in the garage. There are different varieties of bats—wood and metal. Skis are no longer just for swooshing down a hill: there are cross-country skis, downhill skis, speed skis, hotdogging skis and, of course, water skis.

Americans spend their money on a wide variety of shiny new sporting goods. Whether they are used for a daily exercise regimen or occasional entertainment, by a dedicated enthusiast or a "weekend warrior," they are an important and integral part of the American lifestyle.

Golf Clubs

If we take a peek around the average garage, we're certain to find a pair of golf clubs.

Certain? Yes, indeed. In 1989, for example, Americans spent more than $3 billion on equipment and over $10 billion on related goods and services—which seems to indicate that everyone is practicing the Johnny Carson swing.

Footballs

Since the end of World War II, every pro touchdown, field goal, and extra point has been made by a Wilson football. So has every fumble and every reception. And what about all the bonding that Wilson football has provided between father and son?

Footballs are a common sight in the American garage—and very few objects present such a classic, all-American silhouette. All the more surprising to learn that Wilson is owned by a corporation in Finland. However, all Wilson's footballs are still manufactured in Ada, Ohio, a mid-America town with the credo, "We're the football capital of the world."

Tennis Rackets

Until about fifteen years ago, tennis rackets were made from wood. Then more exotic materials started to appear. Metal, aluminum and, more recently, graphite tennis rackets are now common.

It might cost 10 to 20 percent more to purchase a racket at a pro shop, but there are some definite advantages. A pro can offer expert advice and assess your physical characteristics and your game. They also offer service and advice after you make your purchase, whether you choose a top-of-the-line model that costs between $200 and $250, or a prestrung model for around $30 to $50.

American Buying Pattern

- Sporting goods sales continue to grow. Sales were up 2.4 percent in 1991.
- In 1991, Americans purchased $30.3 billion worth of sporting goods, up from $29.6 billion the previous year.
- Sales of home fitness equipment exceeded $2 billion in 1991.
- Sales of athletic and sports clothing reached $12.05 billion in 1991.

SPORTING GOODS

100% American made and owned:

GOLF CLUBS
- Hillerich & Bradsby
- Titleist
- Lynx
- Northwestern

SPORT BALLS
- Rawlings® NCAA® Football
- Penn Tennis Balls
- Penn Racquetballs

BASEBALL GLOVES/BATS
- Nokona Glove
- Rawlings "Gold Glove"
- Hillerich & Bradsby (bats)
- Easton Sports (bats)
- Rawlings Adirondack® Bat

American-owned, and over 50% American parts and/or labor:

SPORT BALLS
- Regent® Tetherball Set

American-owned, using less than 50% American parts and/or labor:

TENNIS RACQUETS
- MAG RAQ® (1–800–4–MAD)
- ZeBest (800–272–7279)
- Gamma Sports (800–333–0337)

SPORT BALLS
- Regent Soccer Ball
- Rawlings Basketball
- Rawlings Baseball
- Franklin Baseball
- Franklin Soccer Ball
- Franklin Basketball

BASEBALL GLOVES/BATS
- Louisville Slugger® Bat (Hillerich & Bradsby/some stock)
- Rawlings Lite Tote® Glove
- Franklin
- Regent®

Foreign-owned, using American parts and/or labor:

GOLF CLUBS
- Dunlop Illusion
- Wilson® Prestige
- Wilson® Pro-Staff
- Mizuno Tour XP
- Spalding Superflite II
- Spalding Executive
- McGregor
- Taylor

SPORT BALLS
- Wilson®Football
- Wilson® NFL Jets™ Football
- Spalding Youth Football
- Spalding Super Flite Golf balls
- Spalding Tetherball Set

BASEBALL GLOVES/BATS
- Wilson® Optima Glove

Foreign-owned, foreign parts and/or labor:

TENNIS RACQUETS
- Wilson
- Head
- Yonex
- Dunlop
- Spalding
- Prince
- Rossignol
- Fisher
- Vokl
- Pro-Kennex
- Donnay

GOLF CLUBS
- Mizuno
- Kennex Infinity

SPORT BALLS
- Wilson® Basketball
- Wilson® Official Baseball
- Spalding Basketball
- Aviva Soccer Ball
- Adidas Soccer Ball
- Molten® Soccer Ball
- Mikasa® Volleyball

BASEBALL GLOVES/BATS
- Wilson®
- Minzo® Super Flex Glove

GARDENING TOOLS

The care and feeding of American gardens is a big industry. It consists of lawn mowers, tillers, trimmers, shredders, leaf blowers, watering hoses, sprinklers, fertilizers, and other "turf maintenance" products. Many of these products bear American logos, but are foreign made. There are, however, strictly "Made in the U.S.A." products out there. For example, Melnor, located in Monachie, New Jersey, makes a nice variety of water-sprinkling devices for your thirsty lawn. Waterworks, of Waco, Texas, makes garden hoses to spray the bushes and wash the car. Workforce, a company in Girard, Pennsylvania, makes high-quality shovels, rakes, and hoes. Fertilizers and lawn seeds are all made in America. Federal law prevents the importation of turf maintenance products into the United States.

Lawn Maintenance

There are 94 million American households, and in 61 million of them there's a lawn to mow. The average household spends 30 hours per year doing this loved or loathed chore. Not much time, when you consider that there are more than 14 million acres of lawns in our country.

Today, American brand-name lawn mowers dominate the field (no pun intended!). You can mow your lawn and show your patriotism at the same time, because the top-selling quality mowers are assembled in America and fit conveniently in the garage. Most brands are as American as apple pie, and have been around just as long: Sears, Homelite, Snapper, and John Deere.

American Buying Pattern

- Americans bought 6.8 million new lawn mowers in 1990, including 1.1 million riding mowers.
- The average walk-behind lawn mower will last 6 years.
- In 1990, approximately 65.7 percent of American households owned a gasoline-driven lawn mower.

LAWN CARE

100% American made and owned:

LAWNMOWERS
- Sears 3.5 HP Deluxe push-type
- Sears Craftsman II 5.0 HP power front drive
- Sears Craftsman 3.5 HP power front drive
- Sears Companion Belt Drive
- Lawn-Boy® 4.0 HP Deck Lawn Mower
- Lawn-Boy® 4.0 HP Self-propelled
- Troy-Bilt® 5.0 HP power propelled
- Rally 22-inch rear bagger
- Craftsman 12.5 HP 6-speed 38-inch riding mower
- Craftsman II 18 HP 44-inch garden tractor

LAWN CARE MISCELLANEOUS
- Melnor lawn sprinkler
- Craftsman Oscillating lawn sprinkler
- Craftsman ⅝-inch x 100 foot rubber garden hose
- Craftsman 26-inch lawn/leaf sweeper
- Craftsman poly leaf rake
- Suncoast hose reel cart
- Impulse Sled-based sprinkler
- Scotts Turf Builder
- Sterns Miracle Gro Products
- Moisture Master 50 foot soaker hose
- True Temper® Round Point Shovel, Square Point Shovel

American-owned, and over 50% American parts and/or labor:

LAWNMOWERS
- Troy-Bilt™ 12.0 HP lawn tractor
- Craftsman 10 HP 30-inch riding mower

LAWN CARE MISCELLANEOUS
- Ortho Weed B Gon
- Suncoast 18-port oscillating sprinkler/time
- Craftsman Contractor/Homeowner wheelbarrow
- True Temper® Lawn Rakes

(continued)

American-owned, using less than 50% American parts and/or labor:

LAWNMOWERS
- Black & Decker® Electric lawn mower #M100

LAWN CARE MISCELLANEOUS
- Rain Bird oscillating sprinkler
- Spike sprinkler
- Melnor Deluxe Water Saver sprinkler
- Gardena® oscillating sprinkler Grande

Foreign-owned, using American parts and/or labor:

- Murray 3.75 HP 22-inch walk behind
- Honda HRS 21 walk behind
- Honda Harmony 215 walk behind
- Honda Hydrostatic 4515 Riding mower
- Honda Hydrostatic 3011 Riding mower

Foreign-owned, foreign parts and/or labor:

LAWNMOWERS
- Kubota 5 HP rear-bag
- Kubota 13.5 HP 40-inch lawn tractor

TRIMMERS, BLOWERS, AND SHREDDERS

Trimming the shrubs and bushes around your home can be efficient and safe with Black & Decker's 22-inch Heavy Duty Trimmer. Before you can fire up the double-edged blade system (which cuts 3,300 strokes per minute in both directions), you'll need to defeat the safety lock-off switch, designed to prevent accidental start-up. This American-made trimmer also features an AutoStop Blade System to prevent injury during use.

Make mulch out of your clippings with the Craftsman 12-amp Electric Chopper/Shredder. Lay it on its side and rake your lawn and garden debris directly into the hopper. The hardened steel blades will make short work of turning your debris into mulch, for around $400.

Any final cleanup can be handled neatly with a small blower. Craftsman's hand-held Electric Power Blower creates a 110 mph velocity from its 1 horsepower motor. Protected by a high impact plastic housing, this American-made wind machine sells for around $40.

American Buying Pattern

- Tomatoes are grown by 94 percent of American backyard gardeners.
- In 1990, Americans spent $6.4 billion on their lawns.
- In 1990, Americans spent roughly $2.1 billion on lawn and garden appliances.

TRIMMERS, BLOWERS, AND SHREDDERS

100% American made and owned:

- Craftsman® 12-amp Electric Chopper/Shredder
- Craftsman® Electric Power Blower
- Black & Decker® 1.5 HP Heavy Duty Edger
- Black & Decker® 22-inch Heavy-Duty Trimmer
- Black & Decker® 16-inch Hedge Trimmer
- Black & Decker® Cordless Grass Shears
- Homelite® 17-inch Cut Dual line trimmer
- Toro® Heavy-Duty Rake-O-Vac®
- Toro® 8-inch and 14-inch Heavy Duty trimmer

American-owned, and over 50% American parts and/or labor

American-owned, using less than 50% American parts and/or labor

Foreign-owned, using American parts and/or labor:

- Weed Eater® Tap-N-Go® Trimmers (10-inch, 12-inch, 14-inch)
- Weed Eater® Gas Trimmer with Blade (HP305B, HP 30T)
- Weed Eater® Electric Blower/Vac (2560, 2510)
- Weed Eater® 12-inch Electric Power Trimmer

Foreign-owned, foreign parts and/or labor

HAND TOOLS AND POWER TOOLS

Frederick T. Stanley began manufacturing wrought-iron hardware in 1843, using the first steam engine in New Britain, Connecticut. Today, America's largest manufacturer of quality tools and hardware, the Stanley Works Company, is still headquartered in New Britain, and they will celebrate their 150th year in business in 1993. Long synonymous with "Made in the U.S.A.," Stanley manufactures a wide variety of products—tape measures, drills, bits, screwdrivers, levels, planes, chisels, hammers, hot glue guns, door systems, hooks, handles, brackets, latches, timers, remote switches, and motion detectors, to name a few—more than 2,000 products that are sold in stores all over America at moderate prices.

Another source of American-made tools is Sears, which has long been known for its American-made Craftsman line, backed by a lifetime warranty. This year, Sears has implemented a new marketing plan that not only saves the company money, but helps save the environment. The first products affected by their three-year effort to eliminate unnecessary packaging are hand tools. Screwdrivers, chisels, wrenches, and pliers will hang from new displays in the stores, saving the company the cost of some 78 tons of polypropylene packaging. In 1992 alone, Sears expects to save $5 million—as well as preserve some valuable landfill space!

There's a "right" tool for every job, and sometimes the primary quality that makes a tool "right" is the fact that it is electrically powered. When you need a power tool, it pays to look for American products, which have a well-deserved reputation for quality, durability, and dependability.

A recent market trend is toward giant home improvement supply stores, which cater to the needs of the 'do-it-yourself" homeowner. These stores offer an amazingly varied selection of domestic and foreign power tools. When you're shopping, take the time to check the labels for American-made power tools. According to craftspeople and consumer products analysts, you'll be glad you did.

One of the top brands is Milwaukee, known for its excellent engineering and competitive pricing. Its Magnum Hole-Shooter drill is made in America. Sears sells its popular Craftsman line of power tools, which are known for their durability and reliability. To make painting faster and easier, check out Wagner's PowerRoller and PowerPainter. Porter-Cable manufactures top-quality vibrating sanders and belt sanders, ranging in price from $100 to around $400. Other quality American-made brands include Ingersoll-Rand, Delta, and Stanley.

American Buying Pattern

- Shipments of power tools are expected to surpass $2 billion in 1992.
- The professional-grade tool market in the United States represents $1 billion in sales each year.
- Exports of American power tools reached $550 million in 1990.

HAND TOOLS AND POWER TOOLS

100% American made and owned:

- Craftsman® screwdrivers, pliers, adjustable wrenches, punches and chisels
- Craftsman® ½-inch drive, flex-head ratchet
- Craftsman® ⅜-inch drive, socket wrench set
- Craftsman® ¼-inch/⅜-inch drive, socket wrench set
- Craftsman® ½-inch drive torque wrench
- American Tool Hand Tools
- Channelock Hand Tools
- Eastwing hammers, prybars, hatchets, picks
- Stanley® Deckmaster™ Hickory Hammer
- Stanley® Powerlock™ Top Read Rule 12-foot
- Stanley® Leverlock Power Return Rule ¾-inch x 16-foot
- Lufkin® 1-inch x 25-foot Tape Measure
- Stanley® 12-inch Snips
- Vaughn hammers, picks, hatchets
- Wiss® Metalmaster® Snips, Metal Cutting Snips
- Skil® Skilsaw® Pivot Foot Circular Saw
- Black & Decker® ⅜-inch Holgun® Drill
- Black & Decker® Palm-Grip Sander
- Craftsman® Electric Stapler/Nailer
- Craftsman® ⅜-inch Drill with Keyless Chuck
- Craftsman® ¼ Sheet Finishing Sander
- Craftsman® 7¼-inch Circular Saw
- WEN Power Tools
- Milwaukee Power Tools
- Porter-Cable Power Tools
- Wagner PowerScraper, PowerRoller

(continued)

American-owned, and over 50% American parts and/or labor:

- Craftsman® ½-inch drive, ratchet
- Craftsman® Microtork® torque wrench
- Stanley® Workmaster® Hickory Hammer
- Stanley® Workmaster® Steel Hammer
- Stanley® Block Plane
- DeWalt® ⅜-inch Heavy Duty Drill

American-owned, using less than 50% American parts and/or labor:

- Skil® Professional Electro Mechanical Hammer
- Craftsman® 4½-inch Disc Grinder
- Black & Decker® 6.0 Volt Drill/Driver
- Black & Decker® Cordless Ranger
- Craftsman® In-Line Screwdriver
- Craftsman® ⅜-inch Cordless/Rechargeable Drill/Driver

Foreign-owned, using American parts and/or labor:

- Ames Tools
- Weber-Knapp Company
- AEG Power Tool Corp.
- Makita Cordless Driver Drill
- Makita Finishing Sander
- Makita ⅜-inch Cordless Drill
- Makita 7¼-inch Circular Saw
- Grashe USA
- Holz-Her US Inc.
- Rex Tool Corp.

Foreign-owned, foreign parts and/or labor:

- Fuller Nut Drivers
- Hitachi Power Tools
- Bosch Power Tools
- Jorgensen
- Roper
- SKF Tools
- Traub Tools

BARBECUE GRILLS

George Stephen is the man generally credited with "inventing" the modern-day barbecue grill. As an employee of Weber Brothers Metal Works, Stephens worked in fabrication and sales. When Mr. Stephens wanted a better barbecue grill, he selected two spun metal shapes being produced by the company for a product unrelated to a grill. When assembled, they resembled a kettle-covered charcoal grill. It was so popular among Mr. Stephen's friends that in July 1952 he began selling "George's Barbecue Kettle." Three years later, the young inventor formed a barbecue division of Weber Brothers and the "Bar-B-Q" industry was fired up. Americans began migrating outdoors, and the outdoor living boom began.

Prices for barbecue grills vary according to taste and the size of one's budget. Weber makes a 12-inch model, the "Tuck-and-Carry," for $55. In the early 1980s, research showed that educated consumers were dissatisfied with the workmanship of grills. A few years went by and grill manufacturers began producing high-priced models. Despite retailers' concern over consumers' reluctance to pay higher prices, deluxe grills sell very well. At the top end, there's the Rolls Royce of grills, the Professional Grill Series DCS 48 with the very serious price of $2,449. Made of heavy porcelainized cast iron and brass, it comes with an individual automatic emission for each interior grill, a restaurant-quality range, a total of 60,000 BTUs (compared with 30,000 in a traditional grill), and a nickel-plated steel motor to power the rotisserie.

Today, there are smoke boxes, "designer" smoke chips (wine, whiskey, and mesquite, to name a few), gas gauges, barbecue utensils, wok pans, warm-up baskets, covers, and range-style side burners. And that doesn't include propane tanks, propane gas, and dozens of other accessories the barbecue grill has spawned.

American Buying Pattern

- Americans spent roughly $5.4 million on outdoor grills and appliances in 1991.
- Approximately 76 percent of all American households own an outdoor charcoal grill, and 38 percent prefer a gas grill.

- On average, a charcoal grill will last 7 years.
- 1991 gas grill shipments totalled more than 4 million units.

BARBECUE GRILLS

100% American made and owned:

- Weber® One-Touch® 22½-inch
- Weber® Genesis® Junior Gas Grill
- Weber® Genesis® II Gas Grill
- Weber® Smokey Joe®
- Weber® Charcoal Grills
- Sunbeam Electric Grill
- Sunbeam Gas Grill
- Sunbeam Kettlemaster Grill
- Sunbeam Deux Gas Grill
- Kenmore Gas Grill
- Kenmore Chef's Delite™ Grill
- Bradley

American-owned, and over 50% American parts and/or labor:

- Preway/Arkla
- Charmglo
- Ducane

American-owned, using less than 50% American parts and/or labor

Foreign-owned, using American parts and/or labor:

- Thermos® Minute Grill
- Thermos® Gas Grill (cart style)
- Thermos® 40,000 BTU Gas Grill
- Thermos® 30,000 BTU Gas Grill

Foreign-owned, foreign parts and/or labor:

- Hibachi 10-inch x 17-inch

OUTDOOR FURNITURE

Today, most reputable manufacturers market durable and chic outdoor furniture. The major key in purchasing outdoor furniture is function. How and where will it be used? Is it practical for you? Will the family eat dinner on the deck? Do you entertain a lot? Do you worship the sun? Stackable chairs and adjustable-height tables, for example, are ideal for apartment and condominium patios.

In the outdoor furniture market, one thing is certain: There is a large variety of quality products and models to chose from that offer convenience, quality, relaxation, and prices to match almost any budget.

American Buying Pattern

- Roughly 7 percent of the 5,800 manufacturers of household furniture construct metal outdoor furniture.
- In 1991, jobs in the metal furniture industry declined 8.6 percent.
- Household furniture exports totaled roughly $910 million in 1991.

OUTDOOR FURNITURE

100% American made and owned:

- Sunbeam® Casual Furniture
- Treasure™ Garden Furniture
- Syroco® Adirondak
- Winston Furniture
- Lloyd®/Flanders All-Weather Wicker
- Grosfillex

American-owned, and over 50% American parts and/or labor:

- Tropitone® Furniture
- Lane® Venture Collection
- Brown Jordan Nomad® Collection
- Woodard Furniture

American-owned, using less than 50% American parts and/or labor:

- Pier I Import Wicker Furniture
- Pier I Import Jatoba Garden Furniture

Foreign-owned, using American parts and/or labor:

- Allibert (Joint venture with Rubbermaid)

Foreign-owned, foreign parts and/or labor:

- Barlow Tyrie Teak Furniture
- Oasis®
- Garantie®

THE PATRIOTIC CITIZEN

Well, here we are. We've gone through our homes and garages and inspected all the closets, cupboards, and corners. We know to read labels carefully and to check out a product's history before making a decision. Whenever possible, we buy American-made goods. We'll never take our American purchasing power for granted again. We *are* patriotic consumers.

But wait a minute! This isn't all we can do. In fact, making changes in our individual buying habits is just the beginning. We can take the same principles that are at the foundation of *The Patriotic Consumer* and apply them to other areas of our lives. When we socialize and when we work, when we travel, celebrate, invest, and vote, we can use our knowledge and know-how to make an even greater contribution to our country. In this chapter, we'll give you ideas and suggest ways you can go beyond being a patriotic consumer and become a patriotic citizen.

TELL THE WORLD

You can make things change! Just the way a tossed pebble creates a ripple in a pond, each of us has a personal sphere of influence that we can use to our advantage.

• Talk U.S. Up

Tell your family, friends, neighbors, and coworkers—and anyone else who'll stop to listen—about the things you learned in this book. (Better yet, give them a copy.) Tell them why it's in their best interest to be concerned about the decline in American manufacturing jobs and the use of foreign labor to produce goods that once were made in the United States. Encourage them to buy American, too.

• Let Retailers Know Where You Stand

Let the sales staff in stores know your preference for American-made products—they really do listen. (Remember, their jobs and commissions are often at stake here.) What they hear gets passed on to the store managers and buyers who make the decisions on what goods to stock and what quantities to order.

• Write to Make it Right

Call or write manufacturers and favorite retailers telling them you want domestically produced goods. Most companies have an address or phone number (often toll-free) for customer service printed right on their packaging. Let them know where you stand.

• Keep an Eye on the Neighborhood

Persuade your local shopkeepers—the neighborhood drugstore, deli, stationers, and hardware store—to offer a decent selection of American-made items. Even service-related businesses like restaurants, dry cleaners, and beauty salons can be encouraged to get into the habit of buying American-made supplies.

Every little bit helps. One person *can* make a difference. What a difference we can make, then, when we all join forces to see that businesses and industry respond to our urgent call for action.

IT'S BETTER TO GIVE

You can use your patriotic shopping skills when buying gifts. You've already seen that there are plenty of great American-made items available. Making it a point to give others gifts that have a "Made in the U.S.A." sticker or label gets the message out in a nice way.

• Give a Gift that Helps Us All

For the holidays, consider personalized gift baskets filled with American-made products for the lucky people on your list. Are you a "flowers and candy" person when it comes to birthdays and anniversaries? In season, locally grown fresh flowers are always a favorite. Chocolates? There are plenty of regional specialty candy companies all across the country that offer quality and freshness at a price far lower than the imports.

• Need a Mag-nificent Gift Idea?

Are you too busy to shop? Magazine subscriptions are always an old standby. *Bon Appetit, Family Circle, Life, Newsweek, Readers Digest, Sports Illustrated, Time,* and *Vogue* are good choices, and they're all still published by American-owned companies.

• Bond in the U.S.A.

U.S. Savings Bonds—a sound American investment—are a solid choice and are available from the United States Federal Reserve Bank and some other banks.

• Support Your Community

There are many ways you can support your community and a good cause and please a friend or family member at the same time—and it may take just a phone call! Just think about what they enjoy the most. If it's the arts, you might give them a gift membership to a local museum or tickets to a play or symphony. Do they have a favorite charity? You could make a donation in their name. Most charities are feeling the pinch these days and can really use the help. Donations are down just when the need is greater than ever. For a list of some common charities, look in the yellow pages of your local phone book under social service organizations.

• Look to Local Craftspeople

Attend local craft fairs and bazaars. These are a great source for high-quality, unique gift ideas—and the profits stay in your community. Compared to mass-produced products, there's something special about a one-of-a-kind handmade object. The price is right, too, since you're eliminating all the middlemen. Why buy a print when you can get a framed original painting or drawing from the artist! While we tend to associate craft fairs mostly with art and jewelry, they offer a wide variety of items. You may find some wonderful handmade goods—everything from baby quilts to hand-knit sweaters, dried-flower wreaths to pottery vases, hand-carved duck decoys to leather belts—all the creations of artists and craftspeople who live right in your area.

• Give "Home-Grown" Goodies

A gift of food is another smart choice, when you're looking for something out of the ordinary. As we saw in the kitchen chapter of this book, there are all kinds of American-made food items available, from regional specialties to traditional treats. Take some California or New York champagne to the party—and bring along an extra bottle for the hostess. Send your child's teacher a basket of juicy red Washington or New England apples. How about some Florida oranges for your friend in the hospital—a little vitamin C with the TLC? From peanuts to preserves, you're bound to find something native that's the right gift for the occasion.

• How 'Bout a Bear Hug?

For something *really* different that's bound to bring a smile, you could send a huggable "Bear-Gram." The Vermont Teddy Bear Company, located in Shelburne, Vermont, offers a wide selection of irresistible stuffed teddy bears that come dressed for the occasion, whether it's for a birthday, baby, or bride. If you're sending to an invalid, special touches are available—such as a bandaged paw. If you'd like, you can even custom-order a personalized bear. And all their bears are shipped in a special carton containing an air hole—so your bear can "breathe." You can reach The Vermont Teddy Bear Company at 1–800–829–BEAR.

• Let Your Fingers Do the Shopping

There are specialty catalogs whose product descriptions will tell you if an item is American-made. Check out the Sears and the J.C. Penney catalogs. If you *really* want to be patriotic, you can find a selection of red-white-and-blue American-made novelty items in the AMERICA! Gift Catalog, 1–800–92–STARS.

• Many Happy Returns

Finally, don't forget to let people know that you'd appreciate receiving American-made goods in return. If you're the one who's getting married, be sure to specify items by (American-made) brand name when you sign up at your local department store's gift registry. And read the next section for some honeymoon ideas!

THE PATRIOTIC TOURIST

Let's spend our vacation dollars at home. In some parts of our country, tourism is the main industry and source of revenue.

Besides, there are probably many places in America you've always wanted to visit, but just never got around to it. Now's the time.

• Relax! Take an American Vacation

Which do you prefer? Plane, train, automobile—how about a bus or boat? You can pretty much take your pick, depending on your destination and how much time you have. There's so much available to see and do within our borders, the choices are endless. The only hard part is narrowing it down. And, the best part, an American vacation is affordable. It can be as economical as a camping trip or as lavish as a cruise—it's all up to you.

• Ride the Rails

If you're in a hurry, you can always take your choice of domestic carriers and fly. But if you really want to see the sights, how about a leisurely train ride on Amtrak? The California Zephyr can take you from Chicago to San Francisco. On the way, you'll get to see some breathtaking scenery as you cross the Sierras. If you prefer, you can ride the Silver Star from New York to Miami, or get off in Orlando and visit Walt Disney World. If you take Amtrak between Washington, D.C., and Orlando, you may even be able to bring your car along on a special car carrier.

For travelers with time to spare, Amtrak offers a special regional "All Aboard America" fare. For one reasonable price, you can take up to 45 days and visit as many as three places of your choosing within a designated area. Children and seniors may be eligible for additional discounts. For more information on routes and fares, call Amtrak at 1–800–USA–RAIL.

• Leave the Driving to Them

Another way to see America is by bus. Greyhound-Trailways has service to destinations all over the country. For fares and schedules, look in your local Yellow Pages under "Bus Lines" for the number of the ticket office near you. Or see your travel agent for ideas on chartered tours. Many organizations and senior groups also offer a variety of charter bus trips.

• On the Road Again

Would you rather drive? How about a theme vacation? Take a tour of several of our national parks, visit historical monuments or check out Civil War battlefield sites. You can contact the National

Park Service in Washington, D.C., for free maps and information on our national parks, seashores, and historic sites. The National Park Service's Public Information Office telephone number is 1–202–208–4747. Or, you can write them at P.O. Box 37127, Washington, D.C. 20013-7127.

Whether you're born to shop or love the great outdoors, there's an all-American vacation that's right for you. Go south to catch spring training and see your favorite slugger up close from some terrific seats in an intimate ballpark. Plan your route around great golf courses—or museums, gardens, marketplaces, roller coasters, sporting events, or whatever else catches your fancy. Roam the back roads and make your own discoveries. Contact your local automobile association for more ideas and maps.

• Adventure: American-Style

If you're really adventurous, there are a number of organizations that arrange backpacking, horseback riding, mountain climbing, and other wilderness adventure trips. The American River Touring Association offers white-water rafting trips on rivers in a number of western states. You can write to them at Star Route 73, Groveland, California 95321; or call 1–209–962–7873. Bikecentennial is a nonprofit membership organization that arranges bicycle trips in North America. Their address is P.O. Box 8308, Missoula, Montana 59807; or phone 1–406–721–1776.

• Teach Your Children Well

Do you have children? A vacation is a great opportunity to teach them about the places and people who make up our country. How sad that so many of America's schoolchildren today don't even know the difference between the state of Washington and our nation's capital! The next time you're planning where to go with the kids, think about slipping in a little civics lesson or geography along the way. While a day at an amusement park can be fun, the memories of a visit to Mount Rushmore or the White House can last a lifetime.

Wherever you decide to go in America, you're not likely to make a mistake. We have so much to offer that millions of foreign tourists come here every year to marvel at our sights. What have we been missing? A lot. You can have your choice of mountains or beaches, deserts or forests, cities or solitude. From Seattle's Pike's Place

Market to the Bronx Zoo, from Chicago's Art Institute to the Grand Canyon—from Broadway to Bourbon Street, we have it all.

TAKE IT TO THE OFFICE

Businesses are consumers, too—big ones. They buy, rent, or lease computer equipment, office furniture, company cars, work trucks, forklifts, and delivery vans. They stock supplies of pens and pencils, legal pads, and typewriter ribbons. There are refrigerators, coffee machines, and microwaves in the break room. Offices need window coverings and carpeting. Employees need tools and uniforms. Stores need display fixtures and cash registers. Calculators, coffee cups, first-aid kits, fire extinguishers, telephones, toolboxes . . . the list goes on. You get the idea.

• Check It Out

Take a look around your work area. What do you see? Just as you took an inventory of your home office or workshop, check out your shelves and desk drawers. What's in your stock room and supply area? The next time you need to put in a request for supplies, see if you can order by specific brand, or at least request that an item be American-made whenever possible. That may be easier if you're the one doing the ordering. If you're not the one responsible for supplies, get to know the person who is.

• Just a Suggestion

Put a note in the suggestion box or write a memo. Leave a copy of this book in the lunchroom. Convince your boss that it makes good business sense to buy American products and supplies whenever possible because it promotes a positive image for the company and a sense of unity with other American businesses. And, what's good for American business in general will also be good for your company in the long run.

• Set an Example

If you own or manage a business, there's a lot you can do to lead the way. If you're involved in manufacturing, you can look to American suppliers for raw materials and component parts. If you run a retail store, feature American-made products in prominent places like end-aisle displays and check-out counters. Educate your customers on the advantages many American products offer, such as better warranty programs and a ready supply of replacement parts. Set an example others can follow.

One example of a businessman who decided to make a difference is Dr. William Lippy, the Warren, Ohio, physician who founded Jump-Start America. This grass-roots campaign, begun in January 1992, set out to support the American auto industry by encouraging companies to offer employees financial incentives to buy American-made cars and trucks. The idea was to have companies give employees $200 cash for buying a used American-made car or truck and $400 if they bought a new one. In a just a few months' time, Jump-Start America enlisted more than 350 companies in 25 states.

WASTE NOT, WANT NOT

The environment—it's a topic that's always making headlines these days. We're constantly being told to recycle, precycle, bicycle. Right. But what's an environmental discussion doing in a book about buying American-made products? Well, it makes perfect sense if you stop to think about it. Here's why:

• Recycle

When we recycle and reuse, we take up less of our own limited natural resources (as well as having to import fewer raw materials), reduce landfill, and cut down on pollution. Remember *America the Beautiful*? The land of blue skies, pristine beaches, and sparkling rivers? We have to live here, so why ruin our air and drinking water? We've gotten too used to being a throw-away society. Even renewable resources like trees take time to grow.

• Reuse

There are going to be times when you may not be able to find a particular item new that's still made in America, or you want something with character, that's made the way "things used to be." This is a perfect opportunity to "recycle" and buy something "pre-owned" or "vintage." Antique furniture is an obvious choice. Feeling nostalgic? Old tools, dolls, quilts, and clothing are often collector's items. There are some music buffs who swear by the sound of the old MacIntosh amplifiers. And, while there are many people who like to restore vintage autos as a hobby, it's not just that classic

Mustang that's getting a facelift these days. All across the country, there are small businesses that specialize in refurbishing and selling used appliances, from Hoover vacuums to Wedgewood stoves. Besides being built to last forever, an "antique" toaster or oven can add a unique decorator touch to your kitchen.

• Clean U.S. Up

Sound environmental practices contribute to intangibles such as our "quality of life." So it makes sense in the long run to use our American buying power to influence and support the businesses that are cleaning up their acts. In many cases, it's much easier to monitor and control the activities of an American company, which must meet stringent regulations, than to know just what a foreign manufacturer is really up to. Also, there are more and more American companies that are making a point of donating a portion of their profits to worthwhile environmental causes.

TAKE STOCK OF YOUR STOCK

Do you own stocks, bonds, mutual funds, or an IRA? Check your portfolio. Where you choose to invest your money can make a big difference. Is your money in American companies and banks? If you're deciding to buy American, doesn't it make sense to invest American, too? You can use the same criteria to evaluate a company you're interested in investing in that you would to evaluate a company you're considering buying from. What is their corporate philosophy? Do they use American parts? Labor? Have they been moving production offshore? Do they provide employees with benefits? Are they committed to making capital improvements and to maintaining modern plants and technology?

• Do Your Financial Homework

Find a stockbroker or financial advisor who's willing to work with you. Then, don't just invest, investigate. Do your homework. Read the prospectus. Check out annual reports, as well as articles written in the various business journals. When you've made your decisions, write letters letting companies know just why you chose to invest in them. Also write letters to companies you *didn't* want to invest in and let them know why.

• American Dollars and Sense

Besides investing in companies, you can invest in our government. When you buy state and local bonds, you are really investing in your community, because the money is generally targeted for specific projects like school improvements and road building. You often get a tax advantage as well. You are also investing in our government each time you purchase a United States savings bond or Treasury note. Did you know that more Americans own United States savings bonds than any other form of security? Maybe because it's such a safe and easy way to invest and offers an attractive return.

There are federal consumer publications available free or for a nominal fee that can give you more specific information about Treasury securities and United States savings bonds. For a list of available publications, ask for a free *Consumer Information Catalog* by writing the Consumer Information Center 2-A, P.O. Box 100, Pueblo, Colorado 81002.

MAKE YOURSELF HEARD

• Vote, Vote, Vote

Always vote. It's a right too many of us take for granted. We're too busy, or we forget to register in time, or we don't think our vote counts, so why bother? Well, each vote does count. There's nothing you can do that's any more patriotic than to get involved in the political process.

• You've Come a Long Way

A good place to start is with the League of Women Voters. Not just for women, this nonpartisan organization is dedicated to providing clear information and educating all voters. They sponsor political debates and encourage citizens to make informed choices. Look in the white pages of your phone book under their name for the local organization in your area. A national membership costs $45 per year. The national office of the League of Women Voters is located at 1730 M Street NW, Suite 1000, Washington, D.C. 20036; or phone 1-202-429-1965.

• Write the Right Stuff

Keep up to date on legislation that affects American industry and labor. Write to your congressman and senator and let them know you want them to support bills that encourage investment in American technology, research, factories, and infrastructure—and whatever else helps create American jobs. You can write to your senator in care of the U.S. Senate, Washington, D.C. 20510. Write your congressman at the U.S. House of Representatives, Washington, D.C. 20515. If you prefer, you can check your phone book for your representative's local office in your area.

The environment represents a potentially great growth industry. The creation and development of environmentally sound technologies in the fields of energy, transportation, agriculture, and manufacturing is a challenge and hope for our ecological and environmental future. Germany and Japan already have a head start. Let your elected representatives know that you want America to be on the cutting edge of this vital and vast economic opportunity. For more information and ideas, take a look at Senator Al Gore's book, *Earth in the Balance: Ecology and the Human Spirit,* published by Houghton Mifflin.

• Community Action

Pay attention to politics at the local level, too. How are the schools in your neighborhood? Is tax money being used to improve education programs and provide job training? Are roads being repaired? Are businesses encouraged to stay and be part of the community? Let your community's leaders know that you care and that you vote. Get involved.

WHAT ELSE?

Find out what others are doing. There are plenty of civic groups and organizations that are active at all levels, from the PTA to the Chamber of Commerce, from labor organizations to manufacturing associations, from consumer groups to nonprofit foundations. The two foundations listed below may be of particular interest to you as a patriotic consumer.

• Buy America Foundation

Another group worth mentioning is the Buy America Foundation, started in 1991 by William Lynott. The purpose of this organization is "to educate and inform the American public" on the value of supporting American products whenever a good American-made alternative is available and the best value. They depend on donations to publish a free newsletter that provides product and other useful information. You can contact them at:

The Buy America Foundation
1044 Highland Avenue
P.O. Box 82
Abington, Pennsylvania 19001
1-215-886-3646

• Made in the USA Foundation

The Made in the USA Foundation is a membership organization made up of interested consumers, manufacturers, associations and trade unions. Their goal is to promote consumer awareness and to influence government policies and business practices. Members receive a quarterly newsletter with information on issues and products. For more information, you can contact them at:

Made in the USA Foundation
1800 Diagonal Road, Suite 180
Alexandria, Virginia 22314
1-703-519-6100 or 1-800-ASK-MUSA

KEEP ON DREAMING

This isn't the end, it's just the beginning. This book isn't meant to be all-inclusive, just a place to start, a way to begin looking at things in a new light. You can come up with your own ideas and strategies. Use your skills as a patriotic consumer and as a patriotic citizen to make changes happen. Rediscover that American dream we keep talking about, and make it your own!

KEEP IN TOUCH

We'd like to hear from you. Tell us what's on your mind and let us know your ideas and suggestions for future editions of this book. You can write to us at:

The Patriotic Consumer
RFD #1
North Salem, New York 10560

THE
MADE IN AMERICA
HALL OF FAME

This chapter is a celebration of the history and achievements of American manufacturing through selected success stories. Throughout this book, we've been telling you about innovative, high-quality American-made products. Many of these products started with a vision, then were developed with hard work and an appreciation of the marketplace. A Great American Dream is to come up with a new or better idea and turn it into a success.

In this chapter, we're going to tell you about some American companies that have shown that this tried-and-true formula still works. Some of these companies have recent beginnings, others are a part of American history and folklore. You probably already know their names. Their stories represent everything that's best about American business.

Pfaltzgraff

The sailing ship *Charles Ferdinand* had a more important passenger on board than anyone could have imagined when it docked in Baltimore on September 17, 1833.

That passenger was Johann George Pfaltzgraff, a 25-year-old German potter who emigrated with his pregnant wife after his village's pottery industry fell into decline. Pfaltzgraff moved to York County, Pennsylvania, where he had relatives. Within a few years, Pfaltzgraff owned a 21-acre farm and operated a pottery business. Of the two, the pottery business proved the more lucrative enterprise.

Pfaltzgraff's success parallels the growth of America itself. By the late 1800s the company produced animal feeders and a range of agriculturally related ceramics. After the turn of the century, the Pfaltzgraff functional home pottery line was expanded to include colorful Art Deco styles. Kitchenware was added in the 1930s. Dinnerware and ceramic accessories were created after World War II, reflecting the country's return to prosperity. Bone china was added in 1989 and a classically styled glassware line was introduced in 1991.

Many of the company's original designs are included in currently manufactured patterns. For example, two highly successful patterns are called Yorktowne and Village, both decorated with forms derived from early Pfaltzgraff salt-glazed crocks. Antique collectors avidly snap up old Pfaltzgraff ceramics. Today's Pfaltzgraff will probably be among tomorrow's sought-after collectibles.

Pfaltzgraff china and glassware are internationally recognized for quality. Still family-owned (the sixth generation!) and the oldest continuously operating pottery company in the United States, The Pfaltzgraff Company operates 2 million square feet of manufacturing and distributing facilities and employs 3,000 workers at its York, Pennsylvania, base. Even the company's recent acquisitions of two other ceramics companies, Treasure Craft and Syracuse China, reflect its focus on the china and glassware trade.

Best of all, Pfaltzgraff products are an attractive American alternative to high-priced imports; with imports, shipping costs and changes in world currency markets often affect pricing. You really get what you pay for with Pfaltzgraff.

And Pfaltzgraff backs up its products with outstanding customer service. For instance, the company has a toll-free "800" phone number set up to answer questions on the care or use of Pfaltzgraff.

For fine china or glassware, think of Pfaltzgraff, an all-American company whose success is the result of its commitment to American workers, materials, art forms and, most of all, quality.

La-Z-Boy Chair Company

The Roaring Twenties was a great time for dreamers. Two of them were the young Monroe, Michigan, farmer Edwin Shoemaker and his cousin, woodworker Edward Knabusch.

In 1927, the year of Babe Ruth's 60 homers and Lindbergh's heroic transatlantic flight, the two cousins abandoned their secure jobs to team up in the furniture business. Like many other fledgling businesses, they used a garage as their first "factory," where the cousins crafted cabinets and doll furniture. Their first company name, Kna-Shoe Company, didn't last long, replaced by the less awkward Floral City Furniture tag. By the end of the twenties, the business had outgrown the garage, though the new venture was still struggling. Turned down by local banks, the cousins found investors in friends and family. The two then built a new brick factory a mile north of Monroe.

Looking to design comfortable furniture, the small company created the first La-Z-Boy recliner, a wood-slat folding chair, in 1928. The entire design for the original chair was based on orange-crate mock-ups. A Toledo, Ohio, furniture store buyer suggested that the innovative chair would see year-round use if it was upholstered. Patented by Knabusch and Shoemaker, the new La-Z-Boy came at the right time—1929, the year of the great stock market crash. Americans needed to relax in the Depression years following the stock market crash. The comfortable chair survived the Depression because of its craftsmanship and value as well as the two cousins' sense of business and showmanship. Adding a retail store and using "Furniture Shows" to attract customers, the company drew them in with acrobatic circus mice and some very comfortable furniture.

Although it was converted to manufacture specialized airplane parts during World War II, the factory returned to recliner production in 1946. Ever since, La-Z-Boy products have set a standard for comfort and quality. The company now manufactures more than 30,000 chairs and sofas a week in more than 7 million square feet of manufacturing space.

Net sales for fiscal 1992 were more than $619 million. Clearly, though they make furniture to relax in, the folks at La-Z-Boy haven't been taking it easy. They do take time to support local charities through the La-Z-Boy Foundation, donating more than $3 million to aid groups such as the United Way, YMCA, and the American Red Cross. The foundation also provided Monroe, Michigan, with its city museum.

Today's La-Z-Boy Chair Company is still headquartered in Monroe, Michigan, with a Knabusch at the helm. Now, though, you can find comfortable La-Z-Boy furniture for the home, office, hotel, and health-care industries. In addition, the company manufactures wood furniture for use throughout the home under its Hammary and Kincaid brands, as well as office systems made by its Rose-Johnson subsidiary.

The current La-Z-Boy line of home furniture includes the legendary recliners in fabric or leather upholstery, sofas based on the company's proven standards of comfort and stationary chairs. The Hammary and Kincaid divisions complement the line. Hammary offers Southwestern-style solid pine and knotty pine veneer tables, wall systems, and entertainment centers. Manufacturing efficiency has enabled Hammary to discontinue importing; all of its solid-wood furniture is now made in the U.S.A. Kincaid offers a more upscale line of dining room, bedroom, and occasional furniture.

One thing hasn't changed—the company's dedication to comfort, quality, value, and America. All of La-Z-Boy's fabric, leather, hardwood, and mechanical components are American because, as the company says, "they're the best." La-Z-Boy is considering exporting in the near future, feeling that "we can help restore universal admiration for 'Made in America.'"

We could all relax if more American companies were like La-Z-Boy!

JBL

Another American success story rooted in the Roaring Twenties is JBL Consumer Products, Inc., an internationally known manufacturer of quality speakers for home and professional use.

Founded by James B. Lansing in the twenties, the company's first claim to fame was the use of its speakers to mate sound with images in the first talking movie, "The Jazz Singer," in 1928. At first dedicated to professional sound and used in movie theaters and other commercial settings, JBL products entered the home arena in 1954. Since then, JBL has been hailed by music buffs and critics for its consistently excellent speakers. JBL manufactures from the ground up. Dr. Sidney Harman, company owner since 1969, says "If you are genuinely interested in putting out a product that is fundamentally better, you have to make it yourself."

JBL is dedicated to quality control. On its 45-acre facility near Los Angeles, loudspeakers are designed, engineered, tested, built, and shipped. In many cases, JBL even makes the machines that makes the parts that make the speakers. Quality is never sacrificed to save production costs. Components are made from the best materials available, then enclosed in stylish, durable cases. One JBL innovation is the use of titanium in tweeter diaphragms for lightness and stiffness.

JBL's unyielding devotion to quality isn't lost on the world's consumers. In Japan, for instance, the JBL name is prestigious and JBL products have won several awards. Since 1980, when the company branched out to worldwide sales, the JBL name hasn't lost anything in translation. Even the company's ultra-premium Everest speakers sell well, though priced at more than $20,000 a pair. Some of the company's recent speaker systems include the ProPerformer Series™, L Series™, and Synthesis Series™.

When it comes time to listen to the best your stereo, television, or CD player can produce, think of JBL speakers, the choice of many of the world's finest recording studios, concert halls, and movie theaters. JBL proves that American craftsmanship can speak out loud and clear.

Stetson Hat Company

John Wayne wore a Stetson hat in the movies and Harry Truman wore one in his forays from the White House. Today, celebrities such as country music idol Garth Brooks wear Stetsons, too.

The Stetson Hat Co. makes all-American hats that are world-renowned for both their appearance and durability. No longer just offering the classic Western hat, Stetson also creates a wider line of headgear, including golf hats and caps. But it is the broad-brimmed Western hat that made the reputation of the St. Joseph, Missouri, based company. The felt Stetson hat is created from felt made from selected furs, combined with a satin lining and real leather sweatband. It's a hat for a lifetime of wear, making the price more of an investment than an expense. All of the components are American with the hats assembled at Stetson's 400-employee Missouri factory.

Stetson hats were created by a city slicker, not a cowboy. John B. Stetson was the son of a hatmaker in Philadelphia, who started his own hat company in 1865, the year the Civil War ended. Initially, the company made traditional dress hats. But a trip to Colorado for his health convinced Stetson that a broad-brimmed hat was needed to tame the fierce Western sun and winds. It didn't take long for the hats to become successful. Stetson's success was shared in the workplace—a company-owned hospital, credit unions, and even baseball fields were available to employees, making Stetson one of the more progressive American companies of the late 1800s.

Today's Stetson hats have plenty of imitators but they're still the standard of the business. Asked why the company takes an all-American approach to components and labor, a top Stetson official replied, "Because that's where we live. The public wants American-made hats."

You have to take your hat off to Stetson, a company that shows a heads-up approach to American craftsmanship.

Microsoft

Bill Gates, founder and president of Microsoft Corporation, Inc. in Redmond, Washington, saw the enormous commercial potential of personal computers before they became widely available.

He parlayed that vision into the world's premiere software company, with 1991 sales a hefty $1.8 billion. Microsoft's DOS operating software has 90 percent of the market for personal-computer operating systems and is the basic software for 80 million PCs. Beyond DOS, its first triumph and continuing breadwinner, Microsoft enjoys great success with Windows™ (a graphical user interface designed to give PCs a look and feel similar to Apple's Macintosh computers), Word™ word-processing software, and Excel™ database software for the Macintosh.

Gates first became aware of personal computers while at Harvard in 1975. The 19-year-old Gates and classmate Paul Allen learned programming with an eye toward involvement in the upstart personal computer industry. It wasn't long before Gates dropped out of Harvard and returned to his native Seattle. He and Allen started Microsoft with the goal of having "a computer on every desk and in every home, running Microsoft software." Gates soon found the personal computer operating system he was looking for—it had been developed by a local Seattle company who called it QDOS, meaning "quick and dirty operating system." Gates bought QDOS for a reported $50,000 and it became the more formal MS-DOS™, "Microsoft disk operating system."

He then convinced mighty IBM to use MS-DOS™ as the operating system on its upcoming microcomputer line. Industry analysts feel that Microsoft made the IBM PC a reality and that IBM's business made Microsoft a guaranteed success.

Today, Microsoft employs more than 10,000 extremely dedicated staffers who, like chairman Bill Gates, often put in 60- to 80-hour work weeks. New recruits sometimes take pay cuts to become part of the Microsoft team. Turnover is low and morale is high in the casually dressed world of Microsoft. To find talent, Microsoft's personnel department scans 10,000 resumes each month, appreciating that America's greatest resource is its people with their ideas and their creativity.

Comparisons have been made between Bill Gates and Henry Ford, with some validity. Gates and Ford each had a vision of his industry's future and pursued it doggedly. Both built empires on existing technology, refining it and popularizing it. And both men have been described as eccentric geniuses. Gates's idea of a vacation is to hole up in the woods with an armload of books and magazines, sustained by rations such as canned tomato soup and SpaghettiOs. His casual appearance and junk-food diet belie a man reportedly worth $7 billion, making Gates arguably the richest Harvard dropout in America. For one Microsoft company gathering in Seattle's massive Kingdome, Gates drove in on a Harley-Davidson motorcycle, leading a pack of 10 high-tech bikers. The crowd of 5,000 Microsoft employees cheered Gates lustily.

They had good reason to cheer. Harnessing American creativity and industriousness to achieve remarkable success, Gates and Microsoft have set the tone for the world's software industry.

Maglite

They've gotten fan mail from troops in Operation Desert Storm, paramedics, outdoorsmen, Peace Corps volunteers, and furniture refinishers. A British plumber even sent a laudatory poem!

All this for . . . flashlights? Not just any flashlight—these are Maglites™. They've been listed in *Fortune* and *Money* magazines as one of the products Americans make best. Company owners Tony and Claire Maglica, owners of Mag Instrument, Inc., simply don't cut corners when they make their wide range of flashlights. From the wildly popular Mini-Maglite™ to jumbo flashlights capable of illuminating a jungle at midnight, Maglites do the job. And consumers have seen the light, pushing Maglite sales past the $100-million-a-year mark.

Maglites are the brainchild of Tony Maglica, the New York-born son of Yugoslavian immigrants. In the late 1970s, Maglica, then owner of a Los Angeles machine shop, thought he could make a flashlight "that was made out of durable material, that had a quality finish—something you wanted to take care of." Maglica aimed his new flashlight at the sporting goods and law enforcement markets initially. The flashlights' outstanding reputation created a broader consumer base, leading to the creation of a whole family of Maglites.

The Maglite family of flashlights, manufactured in Ontario, California, share desirable features such as adjustable beams, a self-cleaning internal switch, and a spare bulb in the tail cap, with a lifetime warranty for repair and replacement of external components. Quality is everything with Mag. Tony Maglica even designed some of the machines used in production. Sold in the United States and abroad, from Japan to Sweden, Mag Instrument flashlights are the standard of the trade. Exports are now 25 percent of total sales. The company "is proud that its products are produced by American workers and are comprised of American-made components and raw materials."

Mag Instrument and Maglite products are shining examples of what can happen when inventiveness and devotion to quality combine in America.

Harley-Davidson

In 1901, two young men got together with two wheels and created one of the great symbols of modern American history—the Harley-Davidson motorcycle.

Those young men, William S. Harley and his lifelong friend, Arthur Davidson, were just out of their teens when they began their tinkering. Harley "bikes" have been the transportation of choice of cops and movie stars alike—remember Marlon Brando in *The Wild One* or Peter Fonda in *Easy Rider*?

Today, Harley-Davidson products range from their two-wheeled standard, now the only motorcycle made in the United States, to four-wheeled vehicles and even clothing. The Milwaukee-based Harley-Davidson, Inc. is the employer of 5,500 Americans. To most of us, the Harley-Davidson name is synonymous with "motorcycle" and the company continues to produce classics. From the entry-level Sportster™, the latest incarnation of its famous ElectraGlide™, to the ultra-premium FXDB Daytona (complete with pearl paint!), Harley-Davidson motorcycles combine the thrill of the open road with unsurpassed quality. Even the Harley's painted parts exceed top automotive standards; details are pin-striped by hand. Motorcycles are tested to limits well beyond normal use to ensure premium quality.

More than 90 percent of Harley motorcycle owners surveyed in 1991 said they'd buy another Harley. A leading motorcycle magazine recently rated the Harley FXDC Dyna Glide Custom as the Best Heavyweight Cruiser motorcycle in the world. The Harley Owners Group, 155,000 strong, enjoys company-sponsored get-togethers such as rallies. A Harley-Davidson drill team, the Victor McLaglen Motors Corps, includes the "Figure Eight Stopping Pyramid" among its 50-stunt repertoire.

These days, Harley also brings its high standards to recreational vehicles, truck bodies, and walk-in vans for commercial use, as well as a popular line of riding and fashion apparel for motorcycle enthusiasts. The name Harley sells: 1991 sales were more than $900 million.

Harley-Davidson is a full-throttle example of American mechanical genius that has shifted gears with the times to remain a tremendous success.

Ben & Jerry's

Ready for a "moo-ving" experience? Put together two young guys, an old-fashioned rock salt ice-cream maker and a $5 correspondence course in ice-cream making and you've got . . . a $97-million-a-year company!

Nobody could write a script more unlikely than the story of Ben & Jerry's Homemade, Inc., which humbly describes itself as "Vermont's Finest All Natural Ice Cream" (though *Time* magazine went a step further, calling it "the best ice cream in the world"). Founded in 1978 in a renovated gas station in Burlington, Vermont, by childhood friends Ben Cohen and Jerry Greenfield, Ben & Jerry's soon became known for its "funky, chunky" flavors and high quality.

As companies go, Ben & Jerry's will never be called shy. Some Ben & Jerry's highlights include "the world's largest ice cream sundae," a 27,102-pound dessert made in 1983, the 1986 launching of the "Cowmobile," a modified mobile home used to distribute free scoops of ice cream around the country, the 1987 feeding of ice cream waste to a neighboring pig farm (turns out the pigs didn't like mint), and the 1990 parodying of Ben and Jerry on the television show "Twin Peaks." Along the way, food lovers and gourmet critics have raved about such enticing flavors as Cherry Garcia, Chunky Monkey, Wild Maine Blueberry, and Rainforest Crunch. Frozen yogurt, Brownie Bars, and Peace Pops are more recent offerings.

Ben & Jerry's provides its 350 employees with great benefits, actively backs environmental causes, and funds non-profit social activities through the Ben & Jerry's Foundation. Even Ben & Jerry's pay structure is singular—top executives can earn no more than seven times what the lowest-paid workers earn. When one production line of 35 workers was temporarily shut down in 1991, all 35 people were kept on the payroll, doing needed chores around the plant and community work. The Ben & Jerry's workers painted local fire hydrants, did yard work and winterized homes for elderly and disabled people, helped staff area food banks, and worked behind the scenes to promote a Halloween benefit for local children's causes. Ben & Jerry's clearly has a heart attached to the bottom line.

When it comes to great American companies, Ben & Jerry's may literally be the cream (or ice cream!) of the crop.

OUR SOURCES

Books

Better Homes and Gardens® Household Hints and Tips. London, England, Dorling Kindersley, LTD, 1989, 1990.

Consumer Guide® 1992 Edition: Consumer Buying Guide. Illinois Publication International, Ltd., 1991.

Consumer Reports 1992 Buying Guide Issue. Yonkers, N.Y.: Consumers Union of United States, 1991.

Directory of Corporate Affiliations: Who Owns Whom. Wilmette, Illinois: National Register Publishing Co., 1992.

Directory of Foreign Investment in the U.S.: Real Estate & Business. Detroit, MI.: Gale Research, Inc., 1991.

Directory of Foreign Manufacturers in the United States: Fourth Edition. Atlanta, Georgia: Georgia State Business Press, 1990.

Donoho, Annette. *Buy American: Who Owns What in the United States.* Box 383322, Waikola, HI., 1991.

Furniture/Today. *Annual Retail Marketing Guide 1992.* High Point, N.C.: Reed Publishing USA, 1992.

Hoover's Handbook of American Business: 1992. Austin, Texas: The Reference Press, Inc., 1991.

Hoover's Handbook of World Business: 1992. Austin, Texas: The Reference Press, Inc., 1991.

Hunter, Linda Mason. *The Healthy Home: An Attic-to-Basement Guide to Toxin-Free Living.* New York: Simon & Schuster, Inc., 1989.

Made in the USA: The Complete Guide to America's Finest Products 1991 Edition. Washington, D.C.: National Press Books, 1991.

Made in the USA: The Complete Guide to America's Finest Products 1992 Edition. Washington, D.C.: National Press Books, 1992.

U.S. Department of Commerce, International Trade Administration. *Foreign Direct Investment in the United States: 1986.* Washington, D.C.: U.S. Government Printing Office, 1987.

U.S. Department of Commerce, International Trade Administration. *Foreign Direct Investment in the United States: 1989.* Washington, D.C.: U.S. Government Printing Office, 1991.

U.S. Department of Commerce: Bureau of the Census. *Current Industrial Reports: 1990.* Washington, D.C.: U.S. Government Printing Office, 1990.

U.S. Department of Commerce, International Trade Administration. *1991 U.S. Industrial Outlook.* Washington, D.C.: U.S. Government Printing Office, 1991.

U.S. Department of Commerce, International Trade Administration. *1992 U.S. Industrial Outlook.* Washington, D.C.: U.S. Government Printing Office, 1992.

Pamphlets

Crafted With Pride in U.S.A. Council, Inc. *Resource List 1992.* New York, 1992.

The Buy America Newsletter. Buy America Foundation. Abington, PA., 1992.

Articles

American Metal Market (Feb. 24, 1992).

Appliance®. Oak Brook, Illinois. (September 1991, Janury—April 1992).

Automotive News.

Consumers Digest. "How to Save Thousands on a New Kitchen or Bath." (July/August 1992).

Consumer Reports: The 1992 Cars. Yonkers, New York: Consumers Union of United States (April 1992).

Crafted With Pride in U.S.A. Council, Inc. "Made in U.S.A.—Job Issue Commercials Show Continuing Strength." New York: The Rowland Company, 1992.

Magnet, Myron. "The Truth About the American Worker." *Fortune* (May 4, 1992).

Marshall, Jonathan. "Many on Welfare Can't Afford Jobs." *San Francisco Chronicle* (May 9, 1992).

Martin, Sue. "Local Food Makes Good." *Amtrak Express* (March/April 1992).

Monthly Labor Review. (Feb. 1992): 13.

Mullins, Marcy E. "Special Report: What Is an American Car?" *USA Today* (March 2, 1992).

Samuelson, Robert J. "How Our American Dream Unraveled." *Newsweek,* (March 2, 1992).

Wall Street Journal (December 8, 1987).

Walsh, Edward. "American Cities Reel From Era of Cutbacks."
Oakland Tribune (May 4, 1992).
Wards Automotive Reports

HOME FURNISHINGS DAILY
September 30, 1991: 53.
November 18, 1991: 51, 63.
June 17, 1991: 69, 88.
February 17, 1992: 45.
April 29, 1991: 106.
October 28, 1991: 60.
July 29, 1991: 59.
October 7, 1991: 3A.
December 30, 1991: 53.
February 10, 1992: 60.
January 6, 1992: 64, A2.
February 6, 1992.

Additional source material came from up-to-date articles in the following magazines: 1990–92:
Ad Week
American Heritage
Better Homes & Gardens
Black Enterprise
Capital Cities Media
Changing Times
Chemical Marketing Reporter
Consumer Digest
Consumer Reports
Consumers' Research Magazine
Cosmopolitan
Country Journal
Esquire
Forbes
Fortune
Furniture/Today
Good Housekeeping
Hardware Age
Home Mechanix

House & Garden
House Beautiful
Metropolitan Home
Money
Mother Earth News
Nation's Business
National Home Center News
Natural History
New York
Newsweek
Organic Gardening
Parents
People
Popular Mechanics
Prevention
Quality
Saturday Evening Post
Sports Illustrated
Sunset
The Family Handyman
Town & Country
Vogue
Woman's Day
Workbench

Trade Associations

AHAM (American Home Appliance Manufacturers)
American Furniture Manufacturers Association.
American Textile Manufacturers Institute
Bicycle Manufacturers Association
Bicycle Federation of America
Cosmetic, Toiletry & Fragrance Association
Electronic Industries Association
Motor Vehicle Manufacturers Association
National Home Furnishings Association
National Housewares Association
National Kitchen and Bath Association
Soap and Detergent Association